Essays from an Old Man

Thoughts about family, religion, humanity, and democracy

Barry Fellabaum

For Jake, Buck, Nick, Jim, Max

TABLE OF CONTENTS

PREFACE

Like most Americans, the coronavirus pandemic changed the way I did things. I did not isolate, but followed the recommendations of the CDC. I complied with the mask mandate a 100% of the time. I limited trips to the grocery store. I avoided large gatherings and unmasked people. I received the vaccine when it was made available to me. My family did the same. We were lucky and never tested positive for Covid-19.

Following best practices to stay healthy was the right thing to do. Compliance had an impact on me as it probably did to you. Many of the things I liked to do stopped. I needed something to do with my time. That's one of the reasons for these essays. The other was a concern about being an old man and remaining viable.

Finding something to write about, especially initially, was not difficult. I grew up in the Lutheran Church. As a twenty-something adult, I wanted more structure in the practice of my faith and converted to Catholicism. The conversion process was lacking to be kind. For the next fifty or so years, I attended mass regularly, baptized my kids, and even was confirmed, but I reacted like a robot most times. I wanted more. To that end, I did a deep dive into the Gospels. It was an adventure, a good journey. It was a history lesson for me. I feel comfortable in saying I know Jesus now.

Learning more about my church helped me be a better Catholic. It also caused me to question—even disagree—doctrine and how the hierarchy tell me what I must do. Several essays deal with these concerns.

I am a proud grandfather! I'm also an appreciative husband and father. I write about them often. Other topics bring focus to the state of humanity and the polarization of Americans because of the vile nature of politics. Education in the country is at a crossroads because of performance and funding. I wrote two essays on these subjects. I truly believe democracy is at risk in the United States. This risk finds a way into several essays.

After writing many of these essays, someone asked me what I was going to do with them. I never thought about it. My intent was to organize my thoughts on topics of importance to become core values for me. The question made me think about sharing my thoughts with others.

So, I did! For the last many months, I emailed an essay each week to family and friends. I received positive feedback from them. I hope you enjoy them too.

Barry Fellabaum

Essay 101

22 September 2020

"The Meek Shall Come to Rule the World"

The title of this essay comes from a hymn (*"Lead Me, Lord"*) by John D. Becker. The lyrics were adapted from a blessing offered by Jesus in the Gospel of Mathew.[1]

On a hill overlooking Capernaum[2], Jesus delivered the Sermon on the Mount[3] to his disciples and other followers. The discourse is a sweeping blueprint to lead us through the challenges ahead.

Jesus began teaching the assembly with a series of blessings known as the Beatitudes. The theme for each blessing is charity and humility. Of the eight Beatitudes, one of the most impactful is "Blessed are the meek . . ." To be 'meek' means to possess gentleness and self-discipline. This person is not violent or vengeful or seeking to exploit others. If I could have a do over in life, these qualities would be part of me.

I'm writing this essay on a fall-like day in mid-September on the 19th anniversary of the attacks on the World Trade Center and Pentagon. The memorials offered today are similar to past remembrances. One gentleman left a somber impression on me. His mission in life is to advocate for all victims of the senseless carnage. In other words, for the "meek" among us. Yes, our government has provided help, but it has been a constant struggle for our representatives to "do the right thing" for the victims and their loved ones.

Why does it have to be that way? In times of crisis, Americans stand tall. During the mid-19th century, we stood up against the ownership of another person. The Great Depression of the 1930s caused hardships of a magnitude unimaginable. There were soup kitchens to feed the hungry. When tyrannical dictators threaten the free world, Americans answered the call. Two-thirds of the casualties on D-Day in France were American soldiers. The United States mainland was never threatened during WWII, yet, we led the fight to defeat fascism. To be called an American it comes with the responsibility to help anyone in need.

The state of humanity in our country is like a boxer on the business end of a Muhammad Ali right cross. Our elected leaders could not agree to provide help to the millions out of work during the global pandemic. Families were being evicted from their homes because they couldn't pay the rent. Images of shanty towns called "Hooverville" during the Great Depression appeared before our eyes. The 2020 presidential election created an atmosphere where neighbors no longer act civil to each other. We were on the

---

[1] **[Mt 5:5]** *"Blessed are the meek, for they will inherit the land."*

[2] Capernaum is located on the northern shore of the Sea of Gailee.

[3] **[Mt 5:1-7:29]**

precipice of a cataclysmic event with an outcome that could change the world as we know it. All because we can't get along! It's time to do as Jesus asks: "*. . . As I have loved you, so you also should love one another*".[4]

Will the 'meek' ever rise to prominence? I hope. A place to start is with the blessings Jesus shared that day on a hill near the Sea of Galilee a long time ago.

---

[4] **[Jn 13:34]**

Essay 102

22 November 2020

A Compassionate Heart

Jesus said: "*. . . What you did not do for one of these least ones, you did not do for me.*"[5]

I hear the message loud and clear. It is my duty to help the hungry, the lady needing a little help to cross the street, the kid without a warm jacket in winter; even the obnoxious neighbor. How am I doing? Not so good; maybe a D⁺.

Why is that? During special times like Thanksgiving and Christmas I do okay. You probably do as well. What triggers our compassion during these times? Maybe it's the Salvation Army soldier stationed at grocery stores next to a kettle hoping for a little cash to help the less fortunate. Or, maybe it is the effort by groups like Toys for Tots collecting gifts for kids that receive nothing on Christmas morning. Or, maybe, just maybe, that's is the real us!

As the calendar flips to a new year, we also move on. That lady from earlier will cross the street again. The neighbor didn't suddenly experience an epiphany. Too bad our empathy is not sustainable beyond holidays.

We keep in frequent contact with our family and close friends; do things for them. What if a friend has not returned your call as expected; do you call, maybe visit to make sure things are okay? I'm sure you do. What about the guy living down the street, do you do the same for him? I hope. Extending a little kindness to others is the right thing to do.

Compassion for others is not limited to the big things like providing food to the hungry. It's the little things that make the difference. Here's a thought, the next time you are out and about and encounter a stranger doing the same thing as you; make eye contact, smile and say hello.

The "real me", an interesting thought. I remember a trip home when the kids were young. We were downtown on a Saturday morning just walking around hoping to run into an old friend or two. We did that and more. It was a special day. As we started back to Aunt Mel's, Jack said to me, "Dad, do you know everyone in West Newton?" I thought for a moment, and said, "I think I do." That's the real me!

Sometimes I forget I am that person from West Newton when the circumstances call for it. With each passing year I get a little better.

The Gospel of Luke gave us the tale of the Good Samaritan to demonstrate the meaning of charity and mercy. A future essay explores the Good Samaritan parable, but for now, here's a preview. When a scribe asked Jesus "who is my neighbor", he told a story

---

[5] **[Mt 25:45]**

about a gravely injured man on the road from Jerusalem to Jericho. Two travelers pass the man without slowing even a step. A third, stop and rendered help. Jesus asked the questioner, *"Which of these three, in your opinion, was [a] neighbor to the robbers' victim?"* The inquisitor answered, "The one who treated him with mercy". Then, Jesus said, *"Go and do likewise"* [6].

"Go and do likewise"! Nothing more needs to be said.

---

[6] [Lk 10:30-37]

Essay 103

2 April 2021

Following Jesus

Jesus said: *"Whoever wishes to come after me must deny himself, take up his cross, and follow me"[7]*. This edict seems clear to me. Practitioners of the faith will likely say they do that. But, do they—really?

To Deny

The decision to join Jesus comes with a great burden. To "deny" means to abandon worldly ways and humbly submit to Jesus. It's not easy to reject the pleasures of life that we have grown to enjoy.

Jesus was told his mother and siblings had traveled to see him. He responded by disavow them. Jesus said in the presence of the disciples, *"whoever does the will of God is my brother and sister and mother."*[8] The New American Bible Revised Edition (NABRE) for the Gospel of Luke tries to clarify his meaning of a "family". Jesus viewed family, not as a tribe with genetic similarities, but according to the devotion to God.[9] On a personal note, I have a difficult time reconciling how Jesus treated his family. I have always valued my family in the most reverent way. It's not an either/or choice for me.

During Lent, we are asked to practice restraint. To accomplish it, we forgo something of interest or desire. Is it the same as a kid giving up candy? Maybe, but first, if you were that kid making the promise, how did that work out?

What if we did a better job of explaining Lent to our children and then walk-the-talk with them? First, it's not about abstaining from doing or eating something we like. A better approach is to unravel the tempting of Jesus by Satan, then imagine walking with him in the desert wilderness.[10] The journey is about knowing what is right when lured to do something that is wrong. The enticement can be so powerful we must muster our good energy to ward off the bad.

Cross

Some view the "cross" from a darker cosmos. It is symbolic of the torture accepted by Jesus for our salvation. It also represents the turning away from self-absorption and the pursuit of material possessions.

---

[7] **[Mt 16:24]**
[8] **[Mk 3:35]**
[9] **[Lk 8:21, Note]**
[10] **[Mt 4:1-11]**

To Follow

Scripture tells us how Jesus recruited the disciples. In the Gospel of Mathew, he came upon two brothers, Simon (Peter) and Andrew; fishermen by trade. He said, *"Come after me, and I will make you fishers of men*[11]*."* The brothers complied without hesitation. Later, James and John, brothers and also fishermen did the same.

As the disciples were about to embark on their first ministry, Jesus said, *"take nothing for the journey, neither walking stick, nor sack, nor food, nor money, and let no one take a second tunic".*[12] With this decree, Jesus was telling them to place faith in God to provide for their needs. They were to tend to all in distress while driving out evil. Jesus cautioned against soliciting or accepting compensation. As a parting thought, he reminded them, *"the Son of Man did not come to be served but to serve."*[13] With that charge, the disciples became evangelists.

There is only one way to be a true disciple. But for us, the conversion "to follow" is not a light switch or easy. How strong is our faith? Is mercy at our core? Do we give freely to those in need? That's not all. We must acknowledge our shortcomings and begin to eradicate selfish ambitions.

Luke told us of a conversation between Jesus and a person of means. This man asked Jesus what he needs to do to receive eternal life. Jesus responded by asking if he observed the commandments. He answered in the affirmative. Then Jesus said, *"There is still one thing left for you: sell all that you have and distribute it to the poor, and you will have a treasure in heaven. Then come, follow me."* The wealthy person could not part with his possessions.[14] A true disciple will do as Peter, Andrew, James, and John did.

How do I join the club?

Think of it like joining a fraternity without the hazing. It starts with visiting the group to find out if there is kinship between you and the brotherhood. If the guild thinks you have the right stuff, a provisional invite is offered to become a member. That's only the beginning. There is much to learn and good works to do to earn admission.

I'm ready to Join. I know what it takes to be in the club. Like you, I have some good attributes — compassion for others; contempt for violence and injustice; responsible for my actions among others. To give up everything as Jesus tells us is necessary, well and on my best days, I can't imagine skipping the grandkids baseball games or not watching the Steelers against the Browns to evangelize across town. I will defer joining to another day. It probably didn't matter anyway. No bid would be extended to me.

To walk with Jesus is beyond me. That's the hard reality. What's not out of my reach is to be more like him. I can do that by taking one step at a time.

---

[11] [Mt 4:19]
[12] [Lk 9:3]
[13] [Mk 10:45]
[14] [Lk 18:18-23]

"And that has made all the difference." This is the final line of Robert Frost's epic poem The Road Not Taken[15]. Frost was writing about choices. Jesus also provided us with a choice—deny, accept consequences, and follow him. Frost wrote about regrets. Jesus speaks of opportunity. Frost had the good fortune to explore the alternative on "another day". When we choose to walk with Jesus there is no turning back.

---

[15] Frost, Robert. *Mountain Interval* (1916), Henry Holt and Company

Essay 104

23 May 2021

Profession of Faith

The ☐Niceneᴄreed is a profession of the Christian faith practiced by the Catholic and Eastern Orthodox churches along with most Protestant denominations. The Creed dates back to the first Ecumenical Council of the Catholic Church held in Nicea[16] in 325 CE. Later, it was adopted as a true expression of the faith at the second Ecumenical Council in Constantinople in 381 CE.

The Nicene Creed is at the center of a Catholic's faith. Like any prayer or pledge, it is committed to memory and recited on demand at Mass. During the parroting of it, I look around at other parishioners. It seems like I am in a sea of programmed androids. Sometimes, it sounds more like babble then a profession of our Christian beliefs.

The Creed is more than words; it is the promise we make as a Christian to God. It is about faith and our pursuit to be like Jesus.

I was an android and babbler; that is, until I decided not to be. I would like to share my journey to understand what it means to affirm faith, promise-by-promise.

I believe in:

". . . one God . . ."
The first commandment reveals: "I am the LORD your God. You shall worship the Lord your God and Him only shall you serve." If you agree, you are a believer.

". . . Jesus is the Son of God; the Immaculate Conception of Mary; the Incarnation of Jesus. . ."
The angel Gabriel was sent by God to meet Mary. Frightened and troubled by the message delivered by the angel, she questioned how a child could be born without intimate relations with a man. Gabriel assured her that it could and said, "The holy Spirit will come upon you . . . the child to be born will be called holy, the Son of God."[17]

After Jesus was baptized by John (the Baptist) and the Holy Spirit descended on him, "a voice came from the heavens, saying, "This is my beloved Son, with whom I am well pleased."[18]

Do you need more convincing that Jesus is the Son of God? Some say there are 165 biblical references acknowledging the relationship. Personally, I have never

---

[16] Nicaea was an ancient Greek city in the north-western Anatolian region of Bithynia. Today, the city is called İznik and part of Turkey.

[17] [Lk1:26-35]

[18] [Mt 3:17]

questioned it. From a young child being taught about religious stuff in Sunday School, I have always accepted Jesus as the Son of God.

In the Gospel of John, the apostle explained the linkage of Jesus to God, his birth, and what he looked like. John said: "In the beginning was the Word, and the Word was with God, and the Word was God. Jesus was with God from the beginning. He came into the world different from other babies. Jesus was born, not by the decision of humans, but by God. He was 'The Word' and "became flesh and made his dwelling among us, and we are witnesses of the glory as of the Father's only Son, full of grace and truth."[19]

". . . that the crucifixion (and death) of Jesus was for my sake . . ."
The decision to be ridiculed, endure great suffering, and ultimately death was his alone. He did it for us; to free us from our sins and be forgiven for our transgressions. Too many of us forget the magnitude of what that means. It's the steadfast loyalty only a parent can give to their child. It's the compassion of the next good Samaritan. It our second chance to be a better human.

It has always been perplexing to me how we are forgiven for something and repeat the same mistake. Raise your hand if this applies. My hand is in the air. Someday I hope we figure it all out.

". . . Jesus was resurrected; he ascended into heaven. . ."
In the simplest of terms, Jesus was risen to return to the Father. Spiritually, it demonstrates to the faithful that trust in Jesus is the pathway to eternal life.

Why did it take forty days for Jesus to ascend to heaven? The reason appears in the Acts of the Apostles. Luke wrote: "In the first book[20], [friends of God], I dealt with all that Jesus did and taught until the day he was taken up, after giving instructions through the holy Spirit to the apostles whom he had chosen. He presented himself alive to them by many proofs after he had suffered, appearing to them during forty days and speaking about the kingdom of God."[21]

In the presence of the disciples, Jesus "was lifted up, and a cloud took him from their sight . . . Jesus has been taken up from you into heaven . . ."[22]

". . . Jesus will come again . . ."
If Jesus is to come again, when will it happen? Jesus answers the question for us: *"the day and hour no one knows, neither the angels of heaven, nor the Son, but the Father alone. For as it was in the days of Noah, so it will be at the coming of the Son of Man. In [those] days before the flood, they were eating and drinking, marrying and giving in marriage, up to the day that Noah entered the ark. They did not know until the flood came and carried them all away. So will it be [also] at the coming of*

---

[19] [Jn 1:1-14]
[20] Reference to the Gospel According to Luke.
[21] [Acts 1:1-3]
[22] [Acts 1:9,11]

*the Son of Man. Therefore, stay awake! For you do not know on which day your
Lord will come . . . you also must be prepared, for at an hour you do not expect, the
Son of Man will come."*[23]

The "Second Coming" is all about preparing for our final judgement. We will either
go to heaven with Jesus or go to Hell because of our unredeemed actions. To spend
time thinking about the Parousia[24] scares the heck out of me. It's like the fear of the
unknown. Because it is mysterious, we become a little paranoid. "What about all
those past acts, did I really receive forgiveness for them; sometimes I do bad things
and never asked Jesus to forgive me." Most people simply rationalize the return of
Jesus and believe there is time to make amends. Others are in denial. I'm still trying
figure out my position on that curve.

**". . . the Holy Spirit is a coequal part of the Holy Trinity and adored and glorified
the same . . ."**
Catholics believe God exists in three divine persons – God the Father, God the Son,
and God the Holy Spirit. If that is the case, the Spirit is an equal partner in the
Blessed Trinity. That is what we have been taught to believe. Then, why is there so
much confusion about the role of the Spirit? It's because of the mystery
surrounding the image of the Spirit. Unlike God, the Book of Genius says "God
created mankind in his image."[25] God has not appeared to anyone, but we know he
looks like us. We know Jesus took human form; Scared Scripture tells us that. But
the Spirit, there no physical description except that scripture always identifies the
Holy Spirit with a masculine pronoun.

In the Gospel of John, Jesus tells his disciples, *"I will ask the Father, and he will give
you another Advocate to be with you always . . . The Advocate, the holy Spirit that
the Father will send in my name—he will teach you everything and remind you of all
that [I] told you."*[26] With that pronouncement, I have an "advocate" to help me
through the challenges of life. The Holy Spirit is the wisdom in me to reason and do
the right thing. I can't see, touch, or hear the Spirit, but know he is there to guide
me. Each time the outcome comes up short, the next time I do better. Some say
that is because of a human's intellect and reasoning. I think the Spirit is the reason.

". . . in one baptism for the forgiveness of sins . . ."
Baptism imparts God's grace on us. Catholics are baptized to remove the original
sin from Adam and Eve. Some evangelical Christians believe a person may be "born
again" through baptism to allow us to start over. The Catechism of the Catholic
Church disagrees. The Church believes "Baptism seals the Christian with the
indelible spiritual character of belonging to Christ. Given once for all, Baptism
cannot be repeated."[27]

---

[23] **[Mt 24:36-39,42,44]**

[24] Another name for the Second Coming.

[25] **[Gn 1:27]**

[26] **[Jn 14:16,26]**

[27] CCC1272

To be "born again" is not about physical rebirth, but about a spiritual renewal according evangelical Christians. It is to start a new life with Jesus. The process begins with believing in Jesus followed by the acknowledgment he died for our sins, was buried, and resurrected to be with the Father. The final step is to recite the "sinner's prayer[28]". Although the prayer varies within the evangelical community, the following is a form of it:

> Dear Lord Jesus, I know that I am a sinner, and I ask for Your forgiveness. I believe you died for my sins and rose from the dead. I turn from my sins and invite You to come into my heart and life. I want to trust and follow You as my Lord and Savior.

To be "born again" implies a crisis of faith or extreme guilt over past indiscretions. Regardless of the reason, we should be happy the person has fully accepted Jesus. If the person decides to be baptized a second time, would I object on the grounds of a single baptism? Absolutely not! If the result of a second baptism is a better human, I'm all for it.

I would like to share my experience with baptism.

I am a convert to the Catholic Church. The process is called OCIA — Order of Christian Initiation of Adults. It was previously known by the acronym RCIA. The "R" stands for Ritual. During my conversion, I was not aware the process had a name other than becoming a Catholic.

Today, I believe the initiation into Catholicism is detailed and prepares the Catechumen with a solid understanding of the Church, its beliefs, and doctrines. For me, the practice was anything but what it is now. It was as uncomfortable for me as it was for the priest. I learned little about the beliefs, the traditions, or the rules of the Church. Back to the story.

During the conversion, I was asked by the priest if I wanted to be baptized again. I needed some time to think about and decided to talk with my mother. Her words have stayed with me for almost fifty years. "You are already baptized, why would want to do it again?" Did the priest believe being baptized as a Lutheran was not legit? I don't know or care. Anyway, I did not get a second baptism.

Jesus was baptized with water and the Holy Spirit. Baptism is the beginning of a new life in Christ. The Church calls the scarcement of Baptism "the gateway to life in the Spirit".[29] When we are baptized, all sins are forgiven. Through baptism we receive grace.

A favorite biblical story of mine is the time Nicodemus[30] clandestinely visited Jesus. He asked, "How can a person once grown old be born again? Jesus answered, *"Amen, amen, I say to you, no one can enter the kingdom of God without being born of water and Spirit. What is born of flesh is flesh and what is born of spirit is spirit. You must be born from above."* Nicodemus appeared puzzled by the explanation.

---

[28] An evangelical Christian term referring to any prayer of repentance.

[29] CCC1213

[30] Nicodemus was a prominent Jew of the time of Christ, and mentioned only in the Gospel of John. He was a Pharisee and a member of the Sanhedrin.

Jesus explained by saying, as a teacher of Israel, Nicodemus only could understand what he saw. Then Jesus said, *"If I tell you about earthly things and you do not believe, how will you believe if I tell you about heavenly things?"*[31]

Evangelicals often cite what Jesus said to Nicodemus to justify being "born again". Baptism is more than words and promises. It is the receiving of the Holy Spirit to guide us.

As stated earlier, when you are baptized with water and the Holy Spirit, the slate is clean. It's up to us to keep it that way.   Unfortunately, that doesn't happen for most people. So, why be "born again" to receive forgiveness?

There is a better way.

The sacrament of Reconciliation accomplishes the same thing as promoted by evangelical Christians. Humans make mistakes and should seek forgiveness through redemption. To be truly remorseful for our actions helps us avoid repeating the blunder. I prefer this approach rather than to petition for a rebirth by being "born again".

---

[31] [Jn 3:4-6,12]

Essay 105

10 June 2021

Confess to God

It is not the Catholic Church of the 1950s! There is little to disagree with that insight. Too many Baby Boomers, Generation Xers, Millennials, and Gen Z have either walked away or became indifferent in their commitment to Catholicism.[32] That is not to suggest that these folks do not identify as Catholic, they do, but either don't go to Mass or have conflicts with the how the Church operates.

Gen Z values diversity and considered more analytical than previous generations. They are pragmatic and use dialogue to solve conflicts. A "Zer" believes human activity is responsible for global warming. Their politics are progressive and likely acknowledge minorities are treated less fairly than whites; believe LGB is good for the community. The Church needs to be more accommodating to this core block of new influencers. The time is now to reverse the current hardline policies of Church.

We can draw a parallel to America's quest to land a man on the moon and the work ahead for the Church with young Catholics. In 1961, President Kennedy ambitiously declared the United States would land a man on the moon by the end of the decade. On 20 July 1969 it happened. We had the resolve to accomplish it and a plan to execute it. The Church must demonstrate a will to undertake the challenge to slow the exit of people under 40 years old.

How does the Church get these reluctant Catholics to return? The place to begin is to understand the Catholic population in the United States. A 2015 Pew Research Center survey[33] revealed 21% of Americans identify as practicing Catholics. That's over 67 million people! Other statistics uncovered in the study indicated 43% (27M) of the self-described Catholics attend Mass weekly while 5% never go. Instead of devoting energy to corral the over 3,000,000 that do not attend Mass, focus should be directed at the group (52%) that show up monthly or less.

The Pew study chronicled a group of former parishioners known as cultural Catholics[34]. They are not practicing Catholics. Most of these Catholics say it is a matter of ancestry, culture, ethnicity, or family tradition rather than religion that keep them in the fold. Furthermore, the majority of these wayward Catholics believe the Church is important to their identity.

---

[32] Baby Boomer, b.1946-1964; Gen X, b.1965-1980; Millennial, b.1981-1996; Gen Z, b.1997-2012.

[33] Pew Research Center, "Chapter 2: Participation in Catholic Rites and Observances", U.S. Catholics Open to Non-Traditional Families, Sept. 2, 2015

[34] Cultural Catholics: Someone belonging to a faith other than Catholicism (e.g., Protestantism) or are religiously unaffiliated (e.g., atheist, agnostic or none).

Cultural Catholics make up over 9% (28M) of the population of the United States. Imagine if all of the them return to the Church and actively practiced their faith? That is unlikely to happen. What part would be willing to return? What needs to happen? The answer depends on the willingness of Church to adapt.

There is no magic elixir for the cultural Catholic to return. The reasons are many and vary from simple excuses to serious conflict with doctrine and/or hierarchy. The Pew study found three out of every four cultural Catholics support birth control; communion for a divorced and remarried Catholic (without an annulment); gay and lesbian marriage; and cohabitation. Additionally, married and women priests are acceptable to them. The rigidity of the Church on these hot button issues are serious obstacles foe a cultural Catholic to return as a full participant.

The Pew study provided data regarding the sacrament of Reconciliation. Twenty-one percent of practicing Catholics ask for forgiveness at least once a year and 28% never go to confession. There is a positive correlation between Mass goers and confession seekers.

Why do so few committed Catholics confess their sins to a priest? The likely answer is that confessing sins to another human, regardless if it is a cleric or a layperson, can be a barrier for many eager to reconcile with God. Adults are especially challenged to accept the traditional way to confess.

Peter, the leader of the disciples, became the first bishop of Rome. Jesus acknowledged his status in Gospel of Mathew. What about the successors of Saint Peter and the power to forgive sins? There are no scriptural indicators to conclude this special power was extended to priests two thousand years later. Some generous interpretation of Sacred Scripture attempts to make that connection. Endorsing this view comes from the Letter of James[35] to the "twelve tribes"[36] of Israel. In the verses about caring for the sick, he suggests "presbyters[37] of the church" are needed to offer prayer. In the Catholic Church a "presbyter" is a metaphor for a priest with the authority to act as a commissioned Apostle.

There is another way. If the sinner deems the need is great and cannot realistically confess to a priest, Pope Francis instructs the penitent to make an Act of Contrition and promise God, "I will go to confession afterward, but forgive me now. And immediately you will return to a state of grace with God." There is Sacred Scripture supporting this substitute. Francis provided an open-ended period to seek a priest to confess. Hopefully, the penitent will do it at the first opportunity. Others, inclined to procrastinate, will make sure the time is convenient. However, it's more likely to never happen for these dawdlers. That's okay. The sinner recognized a need to make amends with God and found a way to do it. And, that's good! This news should be welcomed by cultural Catholics.

---

[35] Defined as decedents of the sons of Jacob.

[36] The "twelve tribes" are named after the twelve sons of Jacob- Reuben, Simeon, Levi, Judah, Dan, Naphtali, Gad, Asher, Issachar, Zebulun, Joseph, and Benjamin. Israelites are descendants of these sons.

[37] A presbyter is a leader of the local Christian congregation.

The willingness to support an argument that we can make a confession directly to God and bypass an intermediary is supported in Sacred Scripture. In the Letter of James, the author told us to confess "sins to one another" and stated a "fervent prayer of a righteous person is very powerful".[38] Is this the same as confessing sins to a priest as the Church teaches? It could be if we interpret the passage symbolically. In a literal sense, "another" could reference a confidant or a trusted advisor. However, the Church affirms that the confession of sins to a priest is an essential element of the sacrament.[39]

Paul said to Timothy: "For there is one God. There is also one mediator between God and the human race, Christ Jesus, himself human . . ."[40] These words are strong evidence for going to God to confess.

Regardless of the decision to sidestep a priest and confess straight to God requires us to accept the sacrament of Penance as the vehicle to gain forgiveness and absolution. It is important to note that approval to reconcile without the aid of a priest would need to be sanctioned by the Church. The odds are long for that to happen.

Reconciliation as practiced by Catholics has a mechanical feel to it — do this, then this, and end with this; let a priest be the go between. My intent is not to trivialize the process, but I am not comfortable with sharing my defects with a stranger. The sole purpose for me is to acknowledge shortcomings and ask for help. The way I do it is next.

The alternative to the traditional way to reconcile our failures is to ask for forgiveness directly to God. It is an oversimplification of the sacred sacrament to simply state that we can do this and receive forgiveness. The image of one day someone is moved to ask for and receive from God dispensation for serious moral or ethical failures is too much for most Catholics to contemplate. Nevertheless, that is exactly what we are taught by Jesus.

I begin with examining my conscience. What did I do that was wrong? It is not like a "5 Minute Oil Change", it takes effort to dig deep for the answers. If there is no sorrow for these things, then I'm not ready to ask for forgiveness. But, if there is remorse and a commitment to not repeat the sin, I am ready to go straight to God for forgiveness.

St. Augustine said, *"Whoever confesses his sins . . . is already working with God. God indicts your sins; if you also indict them, you are joined with God. . . When you begin to abhor what you have made, it is then that your good works are beginning . . . the beginning of good works is the confession of evil works. . ."*[41]

Returning to a better Christian life requires me to make satisfaction to God for misdeeds. The scriptures offer no guidance regarding atonement. It is my responsibility to carefully consider the gravity of the sin(s) and come up with an appropriate plan to

---

[38] [Jas 5:16]
[39] Catechism #1424
[40] [1 Tim 2:5]
[41] CCC #1458 (St. Augustine, In Jo. ev. 12, 13: PL 35, 1491).

reconcile with God. It will not be easy to do. It requires thoughtful reflection, trust, and a resolve that the action is acceptable.

How do I know the plan is adequate? I'm not sure. If my thoughts are honest and pure, the Holy Spirit will guide me to the proper action.

Absolution is the final phase of the sacrament. What must I do to receive absolution for sins confessed directly to God? I can't assume it just happens. The best answer for me is to lean on my faith and allow the Holy Spirit to restore us to God's grace. When I don't repeat the sin(s) or become a more compassionate human, then I know the Spirit is working on me.

Do you need closure to the reconciliation process? By that I mean do you need someone to say you have been absolved for your failures? If you do, this alternative is not for you. My suggestion is to ask for help through traditional reconciliation. But, if confessing directly to God is your choice, then accept help from the Holy Spirit. I do.

Essay 106

12 August 2021

"God, now what can I do for you?"

A Sunday homily by my pastor told a story about a little girl praying for the well-being of her family. Her prayer concluded with a question, "God, now what can I do for you"? I was intrigued by the question. My prayers are similar to the little girl — watch over my grandkids; protect Diane, Jack and Bob; keep Debbie happy and safe; help my sister cope with the tragedies in her life. Occasionally, I include current challenges to friends along with plea for peace and the climate.

I go to Mass on Sundays and other important liturgical days. Like others, I never took the time to explore the Gospels in a meaningful way. So, I decided to fix it.

In John's Gospel, he said that "grace and truth came through Jesus Christ".[42] I didn't really understand grace.

In 2015, the nation mourned the lives lost during a bible study class in Charleston, South Carolina. President Obama delivered the eulogy for the pastor and other victims. His consoling words featured a call to our "better angels" to live in God's grace. It inspired me to understand what it means to have grace.

Reading the gospels was like being transported back in time to witness the journey of Jesus. I was in the classroom of a lifetime—seated in the middle row about half way back—hanging on every word spoken by the teacher.

After returning to our time, I became eager for more. How do I get that thing called grace? How do I receive forgiveness for past failures? How do I become a better husband, father, grandfather, brother, and friend?

This is the beginning of my journey to be the best version of myself.

---

[42] **[Jn 1:17]**

Essay 107

22 September 2021

Birth Control

The Pew Research Center published a study in 2016 that gauged the public sentiment in the United States about discrimination in employee benefits, same-sex marriage, and dedicated bathrooms for transgender people.[43] The report also provided statistical data helpful to understand what people in the United States think about the use of contraceptives.

Chart 1 below provides a snapshot of the use of contraceptives by sex, age, and religious affiliation. Overwhelmingly, Americans do not believe contraceptive methods for family planning and health concerns are morally wrong.

Chart 1

Using Contraceptives			
	Morally Wrong	*Morally Acceptable*	*Not a Moral Issue*
Men	6%	36%	58%
Women	3%	36%	57%
Ages 18-29	6%	35%	59%
Ages 30-49	3%	37%	58%
Ages 50-64	5%	34%	57%
Ages 65+	3%	38%	55%
Protestant	4%	37%	56%
Catholic	8%	41%	48%

Source: Pew Research Center, 28 September 2016

The Catholic Church is staunchly opposed to relaxing rules with respect to birth control. The opposition is centuries-old without much support from Scared Scripture, one way or another. This inflexibility contributes to the increase in people identifying as a "cultural Catholic"[44] or simply choosing not to align with any religious group.

The concern to the sustainability for all denominations, and especially the Catholic Church, is the group in their mid-twenties through the mid-forties. Generationally, Millennials and Gen Z make up that age range. According to the data, this group is over 42% of the U.S. population and almost 31% of them identify as Catholics[45]. That is 43

---

[43] Pew Research Center, *Where the Public Stands on Religious Liberty vs. Nondiscrimination*", Sept. 28, 2016, https://www.pewresearch.org/religion/2016/09/28/where-the-public-stands-on-religious-liberty-vs-nondiscrimination/

[44] Belonging to a faith other than Catholicism; indelibly Catholic by ethnicity or tradition.

[45] Source: Pew Research, 2 September 2015.
Cox, Daniel A., *Generation Z and the Future of Faith in America, The Survey Center on American Life of the American Enterprise.*

million real people or 13% of the U.S. population. Unfortunately for the Church, almost 15% of Millennials and Gen Z no longer are devote Catholics.

Another alarming trend is the number of Millennials and Gen Z in the U.S. population not affiliated with any organized religion. That number is 65%[46] or 90 million. Regardless of how the numbers are interpreted, the already departed or considering to leave is staggering especially if Church policies are the reason. See Charts 2 and 3 for generational data.

Chart 2

Population Distribution			
	Born (yr)	*People*	*%*
Gen Alpha	2013+	32,802,100	9.9%
Gen Z	1997-2012	67,358,500	20.4%
Millennials (Gen Y)	1981-1996	72,588,300	21.9%
Gen X	1965-1980	65,240,100	19.7%
Baby Boomers	1946-1964	70,999,500	21.5%
Silent	1928-1945	21,879,100	6.6%
Greatest Generation	1901-1927	132,400	0.0%
2020 U.S. Population		331,000,000	100.0%

Source: Statista Research, 06 April 2022

Chart 3

Share of U.S. Population by Generation Identifying as Catholics				
	2007	**2014**	**2019**	**2022**
Silent Generation	24%	24%	20%	23%
Baby Boomers	24%	23%	23%	19%
Gen X	26%	21%	22%	17%
Millennials	22%	16%	14%	16%
Gen Z				15%

Source: Pew Research, 17 October 2019.
Source: Burge, Ryan. *"Gen Z and Religion in 2022"*, Eastern Illinois University, 3 April 2023.

For all of the old farts like me, do you remember the game show "$64,000 Question"? If not, here's how it worked. Contestants answered general knowledge questions and earned money for the correct answers. Follow-up questions increased in difficulty and the money doubled with each correct answer. The final question had a top prize of $64,000. In 2023 dollars that is the equivalent of $700,000. If you told me my $100 in 1958 would have the same purchasing power as $1,000 today, I would say you are crazy!

March 24, 2022, https://www.americansurveycenter.org/research/generation-z-future-of-faith/

[46] Cox, Daniel. *Generation Z and the Future of Faith in America*, American Enterprise Institute, 24 March 2022.

Why this trip down memory lane? Remember Essay #105 – Confess to God? I opened with "It is not the Catholic Church of the 1950s!" Like the shock of a $100 becoming a $1,000, the Fifties Catholic never envisioned a time when someone would question the Church. There may have been some grumbling in the shadows, but no overt criticism. The Church was convinced future generations of Catholics would fall in line just like their parents and grandparents. Talk about a miscalculation!

Imagine for a moment you are perched on a rafter high above the floor of a massive meeting room in 1965 during a gathering of all the Catholic bishops in the United States. The leader calls the group to order and asks a question: "In 50 years, will the faithful still do as the Church commands?" A retired bishop calls out, "Of course, the flock has no other choice." Every bishop in the room stands and raucously applauds. Now, fast-forward to today and ask that same question to a gathering of bishops. I suspect the response would be similar, but not overwhelming. That's progress; however, it too little.

So, what is the Catholic Church going to do about it? Pope Francis seems to understand the challenges facing the Church with younger Catholics. He has implemented some changes, but the "old guard" refuses to yield to a more progressive agenda necessary for about one-half of practicing Catholics.

Contraception is not abortion. It does not take an unborn life. It is a tool available for families to plan for the future. It does not end procreation.

Birth control prevents pregnancy from happening in the first place. With the introduction of the "pill" a man and woman can have sexual intercourse without the fear of an unplanned pregnancy. It did more than prevent pregnancy. It helped women manage menstruation, cramping, pain, and the risk of ovarian cancer.

Scared Scripture does not define the use of birth control as illicit. It does, however, promote and encourage procreation. The modern families, Catholic or not, struggle with deciding when to have children, how many to have, and how often.

How did the Church managed to get at a crossroads with young Catholics? The Lambeth Conference[47] of 1930 approved a resolution called "The Life and Witness of the Christian Community – Marriage". The resolution was a robust condemnation of centuries of Catholic teaching on procreation. Lambeth said it was permissible to abstain from the conjugal act of procreation as long as the motive was pure and aligned with Christian principles. The resolve by the Anglican bishops was to make birth control acceptable. The reaction to Lambeth by the Catholic Church was swift and resolute. With an encyclical letter from Pope Pius XI, the Church officially banned artificial forms of birth control.
Cardinal Pacelli succeeded Pius XI in 1939. He took the name Pope Pius XII. During his papacy the Church navigated a world war, the Holocaust, European reconstruction, and

---

[47] The Lambeth Conference is an assembly of bishops of the Anglican Communion convened by the Archbishop of Canterbury. The conference has no legislative authority, but its resolutions carry moral influence.

the emerging challenges to societal norms. He was a promoter of the policies of his predecessor; however, during an address to an Italian nursing group in 1951, he stated, ". . . husband and wife may use their matrimonial right even during the days of natural sterility . . ."[48] This assertion directly contradicted the prohibition of any form of birth control including the rhythm method during conjugal intimacy when its intention is to prevent procreation. The creaky door of the conservative Church was opening, if only a little.

 Seven years later (1958), Pius XII again weighed in on the controversy. He affirmed; it was acceptable to use hormonal contraceptives as a remedy for medical conditions like the disease of the uterus.[49]

The 1960s ushered in a time of hope and prosperity. A young and vibrant Catholic man was elected president. The middle class was emerging as an economic and political force. A developing conflict in Southeast Asia and three assassinations later, the country and world were in chaos.

As society was changing and becoming more progressive, the Church had its head firmly buried in the sand. Homemakers morphed into working women with careers. The laity began to question doctrine. It was the turbulent "Sixties" – a decade of rapid change.

The Church was slow to adapt to the new normal. To allow the birth control issue to fester, momentum would build, and like a runaway train heading towards the abyss, the Church would be forced to react instead of dictate. Pope John XXIII called for an Ecumenical Council in 1959 (Vatican II) to update the teaching of the Church to align with the evolving nature of modern society.

John XXIII and his future successor, Cardinal Montini (Paul VI), worked the back channels of Vatican II to influence the outcome. They did not want a discussion on contraception. The goal was to keep in place the doctrine established by Pious XI. If their efforts failed, the Council was likely to reverse the ban on contraceptives. The initial session took place in the fall of 1962. The council completed work in 1965. The Council made significant changes to Church doctrine, but birth control reforms was not one of them.

In the 1968 encyclical letter by Paul VI ("Of Human Life") included teaching on contraception. He declared, ". . . Equally to be condemned . . . is direct sterilization, whether of the man or of the woman, whether permanent or temporary. Similarly excluded is any action which either before, at the moment of, or after sexual intercourse, is specifically intended to prevent procreation—whether as an end or as a means . . ."[50] The expression of conjugal love ending in intercourse is prohibited unless the purpose was to make a baby.

---

[48] Pope Pius XII, *Address to Midwives on the Nature of Their Profession*, October 29, 1951, https://www.papalencyclicals.net/pius12/p12midwives.htm

[49] Pope Pius XII, To the VII Congress of the International Society of Hematology, September 12, 1958, https://nacn-usa.org/wp-content/uploads/Pius-XII-1958-Society-on-Hematology.pdf

[50] Pope Paul VI, *Unlawful Birth Control Methods, para.14*, The Regulation of Birth, Humanae Vitae, 25 July 1968

During Paul VI's reign, contraceptive methods by Catholics were in widespread use. A survey in 1965 of Catholic women revealed more than half used a form of contraception; by 1973, two-third of married Catholic women used birth control to avoid pregnancy.[51]

The Church, in 1981 recognized its position on birth control was untenable and endorsed Natural Family Planning (NFP) as a method to manage family size. The USCCB[52] said this method is "based on the observation of the naturally occurring signs and symptoms of the fertile and infertile phases of a woman's menstrual cycle. No drugs, devices, or surgical procedures are used to avoid pregnancy". NFP is promoted as an alternative to artificial contraception and the bishops painstakingly pointed out it is not the Rhythm method. IT'S NOT!

NFP seems to be in conflict with almost 100 years of teaching on marriage and procreation. The union between a married couple was to be pure and spontaneous. Accordingly, conjugal love was to be at the center of procreation. The practice of natural birth control with all it entails is counterintuitive to the intent of the Church.

For the next forty years after American Catholic bishops approved the rhythm method for birth control, SILENCE is the operative word to describe the Church dialogue on the topic of contraception. Too bad.

Contraception is one of many challenges facing the Church. Others include divorce and communion; same-sex marriage; homosexuality; women as priests; and sexual abuse within the Church. The reluctance on the part of the hierarchy to join a serious conversation with modern Catholics risk the continuing exodus of Millennials and Generation Z. The Church needs to find a bridge to these groups to allow centuries of doctrine to merge with the life choices of contemporary times.

---

[51] Gjelten, Tom, 50 Years Ago, The Pope Called Birth Control 'Intrinsically Wrong', National Catholic Reporter, July 3, 2018.
[52] United States Conference of Catholic Bishops

Essay 108

17 October 2021

To Serve

Jesus said: *". . . the Son of Man did not come to be served but to serve . . ."*[53]

We know what Jesus meant by these words. His audience was the disciples. What if we change it up a little and say, "Barry Fellabaum did not come to be served, but to serve you". What's your initial perception of me — a little strange, maybe weird? Let's change it one more time. "Barry Fellabaum came for you to serve me, not the other way around." Would you call me an a%%hole?

The message here is to serve is not "doing things right", but a noble calling and part of our obligation to each other.

The following scenario helps shed a little light on what it means "to serve". A guy is asked to help out at a local foodbank. He responded, "I have a family, the rent is due next week, and if I don't show up for work, I don't get paid. I care about others, but I can't help on Thursday." I'm sure you have heard rationalizations like that before. The guy needs to understand that to provide for a family is service. The challenge for us is to understand "to serve" takes many forms.

The intent with the above story was not to dimmish the importance of working at a foodbank or delivering a meal to someone that may be immured or chatting with someone that is lonely. These folks give freely of their time and are among the best of us.

Remember the draft during the 1960s? The times were turbulent and the emotions matched that intensity. There was a sense of inevitability. Most expected to serve in the military. The choices were to enlist now or accept the call from the draft board. It didn't matter the route, those that served did so honorably.

That is, unless you could find a way to avoid the draft.

Evading the draft took many paths. Some draftees fled to Canada while others faked physical or mental challenges; the privileged used family connections to stay out of the Army or Marines.

At a local VFW, and after a few too many beers, it's likely to hear a conversation among Vietnam era veterans disparaging "draft doggers". They are labeled unpatriotic and worse. I never join the chorus that criticized guys that did not serve, now or back in the day. It was my choice to go. It has taken me a long time to be proud of my service.

For reasons I never fully understood is how leaving the country to avoid military service is considered more egregious than using influence to do the same. Some, not all,

---

[53] **[Mk 10:45]**

draftees fled the United States for reasons of conscious. I admire anyone with strong convictions. Remaining true to beliefs is service.

In closing, there are stories about achieving the impossible. An athlete is an example. Athletes compete to accomplish a goal. Sometimes the task seems hopeless yet the human spirit takes over and what appeared to be a lost cause suddenly becomes possible. Is it a spiritual intervention or something else? The point is by believing in a righteous endeavor, we are able to reach deep within our being to do the improbable for the greater good.

That's what we do, serve others for the greater good of humanity.

Essay 109

13 May 2022

Integrity

John Fisher was a staunch defender of papal supremacy during the English Reformation during the 16th century. Fisher was an English Catholic bishop and served as the Chancellor of the University of Cambridge. He refused to recognize Henry VIII as the head of the Church of England. The Catholic cleric was imprisoned and eventually executed for his stance.

In a homily recently, Father Steve used a quote from Bishop Fisher for us to contemplate; "What will it profit a man to gain the whole world, and to lose his own soul?"[54] For me, this reflection speaks to principle and integrity. Since the quote was offered during Mass, I decided to search the scriptures for its source.

The Gospels include passages similar to the Fisher quote. Jesus said, *"What profit would there be for one to gain the whole world and forfeit his life?"*[55] Comparing the two is a distinction without a difference. Jesus used the expression to convince his future disciples to deny self, take up their cross, and follow him. Fisher's use of it was at the core of his being. His actions are a model for all of us to follow.

Peter Drucker was a pioneer in management theory. Of the many contributions Drucker made to corporate America, the phrase coined by him to "do the right thing" became a bedrock for me in my personal and professional life. When confronted with a difficult decision, I always think about what is right before moving on. I ask my family to do the same.

Unfortunately, too many of us lack the resolve to "do the right thing". I was one of the "us" earlier in my life. Regrets, of course, but I made changes to lead a more principled life. It's not an insurmountable obstacle.

Jesus said: **"No one can serve two masters. He will either hate one and love the other, or be devoted to one and despise the other. . ."**[56]. People with good hearts, but ethical challenges should internalize these words. It is not a binary choice when asked to "do the right thing". We always have options, choose wisely.

Martin Luther King Jr , in an address to a group of clergy and lay people about American involvement in Vietnam, he offered, "there comes a time when one must take a position that is neither safe, nor political, nor popular, but one must take it because one's conscience tells one that it is right".[57] God advice!

---

[54] Lewis, "The Life of Dr. John Fisher, Vol II", London, 1855, 150.

[55] [Mathew 16:26]

[56] [Mathew 6:24]

[57] "A Proper Sense of Priorities", February 6, 1968, Washington, D.C.

Essay 110

26 August 2022

Abortion

My motivation for writing this essay was the attack by the United States Conference of Catholic Bishops (USCCB) on Joe Biden for supporting a woman's right to make a personal decision about an unborn child.   The clerics wanted to withhold communion from him because of his belief and not because he favors abortion. By all accounts, he is a committed Catholic.

Abortion is wrong. I have three children and five grandkids that call me "Pap-Pap". I can't imagine; don't want to even think about not having them in my life. That is me speaking. I will not, speak for you.

God gave me the faculty to learn, to explore, and to find things out for myself. Taking the life of an unborn child for no other reason than it is not wanted is one of the most consequential decisions of a lifetime. I made my choice; however, it is not for me to make it for you. In political terms, that makes me "pro-choice". What an absurd label! I already stated my position; yet, some choose to pin a tag on me. Tag me, if you must, but say of me that I leave personal decisions to you to make.

The people opposed to abortion make the issue about morality. If you respect a woman's right to make a personal decision, then the implication is that you are immoral and on the wrong side. If you agree with the anti-abortion movement, you are righteous.

Public opinion strongly supports the legal right to seek an abortion (See Chart 1). It is clear from a survey by Pew Research the choice to abort a fetus is personal and should not be left to others to make it for them.

Chart 1

U.S. Religious Affiliation and Abortion		
	Legal in Most Cases	**Illegal in Most Cases**
All U.S. Adults	61%	38%
Catholics	56%	42%
Protestants	55%	43%
Religiously Unaffiliated	83%	17%

Source: Pew Research Center, 10/20/2020[58]

Matthew A. Hamilton, a law librarian in Richmond, Virginia, submitted an article as part of Catholic Voices that was published in U.S. Catholic. He offered the following: "I do not believe every abortion is morally illicit. Furthermore, we do not have the right to unanimously claim that saving the life of a child outweighs the moral responsibility of

---

[58] https://www.pewresearch.org/fact-tank/2020/10/20/8-key-findings-about-catholics-and-abortion/

saving the life of a mother." He described two real life challenges for pregnant women. I encourage you to read the article. Here's the link, https://uscatholic.org/articles/202104/choose-compassion-during-complex-pregnancies/

The Pew Research Center in a 2016 study (See Chart 2) found almost 1/3 of the respondents did not see abortion as a moral issue. Another 15-20% said it was morally acceptable. About 1/2 believe it is wrong. Interestingly, Catholics that regularly attend mass overwhelming condemn abortion. Catholics that attend mass less frequently fall in line with the general public. It's not a stretch to conclude exposure to the influence of the Church has an important impact on how people view the issue.

Chart 2

Having an Abortion

	Morally Wrong	Morally Acceptable	Not a Moral Issue
Men	45%	20%	33%
Women	43%	18%	35%
Ages 18-29	37%	27%	36%
Ages 30-49	46%	17%	35%
Ages 50-64	46%	15%	33%
Ages 65+	45%	20%	31%
Protestant	54%	14%	28%
Catholic	51%	16%	31%

Catholics

	Morally Wrong	Morally Acceptable	Not a Moral Issue
Attend Mass - Weekly	83%	4%	12%
Attend Mass - Less Often	38%	21%	39%

Source: Pew Research Center, 09/28/2016[59]

The Catholic Church needs to pay attention to Millennials and the emerging Gen Z population (See Chart 3). Millennials and Gen Z make up over 40% of the U.S. population in 2022.[60] A study[61] by GetReligion.org in 2022 reported that 17% of the Millennials identify as Catholic. Another 14% of Gen Z do the same. Together, that's more than 43M Catholics! There has been a slow, but steady departure of Millennials from the Church. Issues like abortion, same-sex unions, and divorce are likely responsible for it.

---

[59] https://www.pewresearch.org/religion/2016/09/28/where-the-public-stands-on-religious-liberty-vs-nondiscrimination/

[60] Statista Research, 04.06.2022

[61] Burge, Ryan. *Gen Z and trends in religious faith and practice: Looking at 2021 and beyond*, GetReligion.org, 25 June 2022.

Population Distribution

	Born (yr)	People	%
Gen Alpha	2013+	32,802,100	9.9%
Gen Z	1997-2012	67,358,500	20.4%
Millennials (Gen Y)	1981-1996	72,588,300	21.9%
Gen X	1965-1980	65,240,100	19.7%
Baby Boomers	1946-1964	70,999,500	21.5%
Silent	1928-1945	21,879,100	6.6%
Greatest Generation	1901-1927	132,400	0.0%
2020 U.S. Population		331,000,000	100.0%

Source: Statista Research, 06 April 2022

I go to Mass to make me a better person—simple. I don't go because it's a place to prove my belief in God. I don't go to impress anyone. I go to talk to Jesus and ask for forgiveness for my transgressions. For that one-hour a week, I want to be free from the burdens of making ends meet or trying to survive in a society that is in crisis. Is that too much to ask?

Apparently, it is! I come to expect a second collection to support retired priests or for ministries around the world. I don't hear appeals for those struggling in poverty in Appalachia. The kicker for me happens when the Church calls me to join a pilgrimage to Washington, D.C. to confront elected officials to prevent another human with a functioning brain to use it to make a decision that will live with them forever.

On 24 June 2022, the political agenda of the American bishops successfully overturned the right of a woman to seek an abortion. The decision provided the states with the authority to set abortion policy.

The Pew Research Center published a survey (<u>Chart 4</u>) after the Supreme Court decision on Roe v. Wade. The most interesting takeaway for me was the general public's view on the legality of abortion. In 1995, 60% of Americans believe abortion should be legal. The same survey reported 62% (2022) of respondent agree it should be legal. For more than 25 years, Americans overwhelmingly support a woman's right to make healthcare decisions. Is there any more to say about why young Catholics are becoming disillusioned with the Church?

Chart 4

Public View of Abortion

Year	Legal	Illegal
1995	60%	38%
2022	62%	36%

Here's a little sarcastic snippet for your enjoyment.

Did you go to the party last night? What party? You know, the one at the Old Post Office Building in Washington, D.C. I thought the place was called the Trump International Hotel. It is, but not for long.

What a night! Everyone was there; Moe, Shemp, Larry, Curly, and Prymaat Conehead from the Supreme Court. There was an ex-vice president sitting in the corner of the room waiting for someone to say hello. A well-known congressman was puking in the spiked punch bowl. The good times could not get any better.

There was a black man in a black nightgown sitting at the head table yelling "high five brother" to anyone in shouting distance. A white guy was trying to fist bump a lady in a black housecoat, but kept missing. There was a bunch of short fat guys wearing black shirts with white dog collars smoking Cuban cigars. What a night!

Then, the double mahogany doors at the entrance to the room slowly opened and a man dressed in a toga wearing sandals with long hair down to his shoulders was standing there observing the crowd. The congressman from Ohio, excited and looking to relieve himself screamed, It's John Lennon! No said his soulmate from central Pennsylvania, it's Moses. Nearby, the cool congressman from Florida was rapping with Girl Scouts from Texas, overheard the discussion and said, "Hey stupid, Moses never wore a toga, he wore a red horse blanket to keep warm."

The busboy that was busy cleaning up the puke, looked up and said, "It's Jesus"! When four of the five blacked-robed revelers realized the man in the doorway was the Messiah, they were overcome by the same fear experienced by a deer as a car approaches. Why the fear, all were Catholic. Should they genuflect, make the sign of the cross, or run?

Jesus took a couple of steps forward and said, *what profit would there be for one to gain the whole world and forfeit his life*?"[62] He departed through the mahogany doors. The guys smoking the cigars suddenly had nothing to say. The justices looked thunderstruck. The guy sitting in the corner was still looking for a friend.

Kansas was ready to accept the challenge to overturn the unfettered access of a woman to a legal abortion. The proposal—No State Constitutional Right to Abortion and Legislative Power to Regulate Abortion Amendment—went to the voters on 2 August 2022. The measure would have amended the state constitution to explicitly reject a right to abortion or any government funding for the procedure. Additionally, the state legislature would have the authority to pass laws on abortion, "including, but not limited to, pregnancy resulting from rape or incest; or to save the life of the mother."[63] For me, the amendment, although not the most extreme being considered in states, ranks with the most egregious attack on personal freedoms.

Kansas, a very conservative state, soundly rejected the amendment. Three out of every five Kansans voted to affirm a woman's right to make healthcare choices.

---

[62] [Mathew 16:26]

[63] Source: Ballotpedia

The extent of financial support by the Church to influence passage of the Kansas constitutional amendment is staggering. The following is the activity of the Catholic Church and affiliated groups:

- Archdiocese of Kansas City - $3,180,000
- Diocese of Wichita - $652,130
- Diocese of Salina - $175,000
- Diocese of Dodge City - $5,000
- Kansas Catholic Conference (political arm of the archdiocese) - $275,000
- Local parishes and organizations (e.g. Knights of Columbus) - $150,000 estimate

Add it all up and Catholics in Kansas contributed almost $5M to limit a woman ability to access health care. How many meals, doctor visits, medication refills, rent and utilities subsidies, or crisis interventions would $5M pay for in Kansas?

Should the Kansas amendment pass?

	Yes	No
All	41%	57%
Men	47%	52%
Women	36%	62%

There is a clear consensus for protecting a woman's right to make personal decisions affecting her wellbeing and health. The Kansas rebuff emphatically made that point. Another key outcome was that the people of Kansas rejected government overreach. We expect politicians to "stay in their lane" and pursue the things that make our lives better. They need to stop pandering to the money interests and the loudest voices. The message to them is to "do the right thing" and not worry about the next campaign. The Catholic hierarchy needs to listen to the message sent by Kansans and the rest of America and return to being a "good shepherd" to all of us.

The Catholic Church is not leading in a pastoral way in the abortion debate. Instead, it is telling us what to do, and if you don't like it, too bad. I want for my kids, their kids, and the kids of their kids to feel comfortable knowing Jesus is always there for them. That is the role of the Church—to help lead us to a better place.

Let me leave you with some advice from Jesus. *"Stop judging and you will not be judged. Stop condemning and you will not be condemned. Forgive and you will be forgiven."* [64]

---

[64] **[Lk 6:37]**

Essay 111

30 August 2022

Cafeteria Catholic

Imagine being part of a phone survey on religious preference. The facilitator asks: "If you are Christian and a part of a mainline denomination, why are you a part of it?" After a few responses, it's your turn. "I'm Catholic and I like the structure and discipline." Your spouse overhears you answer and thinks, "Just yesterday you said it was wrong to confess to a priest." The Catholic Church is certainly structured in its practices and rules. However, most Catholics take an à la carte approach to defining why they choose to be part of the Church.

What is a "good Catholic"? For most of my time in the Church a "good Catholic" was someone that believed in God and the teaching of Jesus. Mass was a place to go to grow in faith and reflect on my transgressions; ask for help to make me a better person. It was an hour every week to be free from all the chatter around me. Now, with the Church aggressively pushing its political agenda during Mass and after, my hour of respite is being interrupted forcing me to look for an alternative way to find solace.

I am a "good Catholic" in the ways that are important to me. The difference between how I work my faith and the way the Church wants me to do it is a growing concern for me. As I struggle to make sense of it all, the words of John Bacon, a deacon at Holy Name of Jesus, gives me hope. He said: "A 'good Catholic', therefore, is not one who is 'good' in the eyes of others, but one who is 'good' in the eyes of God."[65]

Why can't I be a Catholic and adapt teachings to fit my beliefs? That sound your just heard are the jaws of traditional Catholics hitting the floor! Traditionalists are committed to a strict adherence to the teachings of the Church. There no middle ground for them. If doctrine says go this way, they go; sometimes blindly.

Some traditionalists subscribe to a discipline known as Catholic Apologetics. The mission of an apologist is to defend teachings, beliefs, and practices of the Catholic Church. The most fervent apologists have little tolerance for anyone disagreeing with doctrine. Apologists call those that disagree "lapsed Catholics"[66]. Surely, Jesus did not show the same scorn for some of his followers.

It is unfair to group all traditional Catholics with the apologists. It is admirable to commit to affirming the doctrine of the Church in absolute terms. It is another thing to be intolerant of those that do not share the same commitment. That brings me to another subset of Church — "Cafeteria Catholics".

---

[65] Bacon, Deacon John. "What Makes a Catholic a Good Catholic?", Catholic Stand, 18 Nov 2019, https://catholicstand.com/what-makes-a-catholic-a-good-catholic/#.

[66] A lapsed Catholic is a non-practicing Catholic that may still identify as a Catholic.

In a 2015 article for U.S. Catholic, Isabella Moyer wrote: "Gone are the days of blind, unquestioning obedience. Gone are the days of conversion by fear. Gone are the days of forcing and enforcing beliefs through militant apologetics with the expectation that doctrinal arguments can be ended with a simple catechism quote."[67] After reading the article, the reasons why cultural, cafeteria, and lapsed Catholics question the direction of the Church comes into focus.

Age is a major factor in terms of compliance with Catholic doctrine. It's understandable why Baby Boomers remain in the fold. This group are children of the Greatest Generation[68]; folks that experienced an economic collapse and a world war. "Boomers" value tradition and the status quo. They are averse to risk taking.

In contrast to seventy-something folks, Millennials and Generation Z are analytical, believe in dialogue, and value individualism. These generations are spiritually conscious, but less attached to an organized religion. Therefore, they are not easily intimidated by the "my way or the highway" approach of the Church. This rigidity exposes a fault line that continues to widen with every controversial issue promoted or backed by the Church.

Over the last twenty or more years, identifying as Catholic as a share of U.S. population is in decline (See the chart below). The downward trend cuts across all generations. The steepest drop off occurred with Millennials. If this trend continues and infiltrate Generation Z, the Church will be at a crossroads. Does the Church adjust or risk alienating more Catholics by maintaining a hardline arrogance? There is good news, Pope Francis understands the challenge and is beginning to change some of the more controversial teachings.

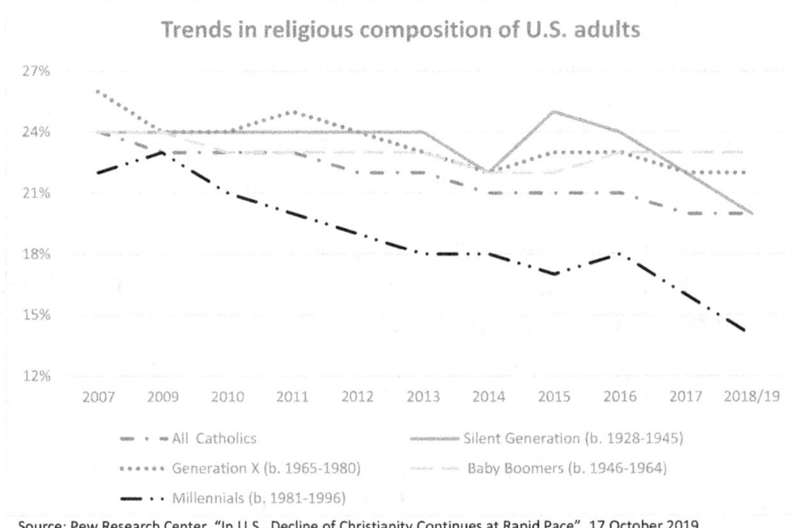

Source: Pew Research Center, "In U.S., Decline of Christianity Continues at Rapid Pace", 17 October 2019

---

[67] Moyer, Isabella R., *Proud to be a cafeteria Catholic*, uscatholic.org, 21 July 2015
[68] The "Greatest Generation" is a term used by journalist Tom Brokaw to describe Americans born between the year of 1910–1924.

What is a "Cafeteria Catholic"? But first, let me share something a professor named A.J. Boyd wrote: "I have honestly never met a Catholic—even among bishops— who agreed 100% of everything the Church teaches."[69]

A Cafeteria Catholics is just like you and me. Their faith is strong. They go to Mass no more or less than you and me. If they are like you and me, why is the hierarchy of the Church along with apologists out to get them? The easy answer is that a Cafeteria Catholic does not agree with every precept of the Catechism, especially confession, abortion, birth control, divorce among other religious and social beliefs.

Catholic Answers[70] define a Cafeteria Catholic to be someone that picks and chooses what teaching to believe. The media ministry broadens the schism with some of those questioning the direction of the Church by proclaiming "Catholics are not free to choose which teachings to obey."[71] With these matter-of-fact declarations, I sometimes wonder if the motive of apologists is to create a "members-only" club.

In an earlier essay (#105 – "Confess to God"), I offered my views on Confession. I believe I owe God an explanation for any bad acts. More important to me is to show remorse for those acts and work to avoid any repeats. My approach to confessing sins run counter to traditionalists and the Church. I must be a Cafeteria Catholic!

I am opposed to abortion, but not to the degree the Church would like me to be. In Essay #110 - Abortion, I said the same thing as here, but included data from the Pew Research Center and other sources on the opinions of Americans on this subject. The generational divide should be alarming to the Church. I must be a Cafeteria Catholic!

When I think about divorce, there are likely more reasons to end a relationship then there are reasons for getting married in the first place. The Church will approve dissolving a union; it is called an annulment. From what I know, if someone petitions for it, the chances are good that it will be granted. Whether the Church sanctions a divorce or not, withholding the Eucharist from a person that remarries is wrong. I must be a Cafeteria Catholic!

Contraception is not abortion. It does not take an unborn life. It is a tool available for families to plan for the future. It does not end procreation. The Church opposes all forms of birth control. I do not. I must be a Cafeteria Catholic!

On the matter of sexual preference or identity, frankly, I don't understand it. That's on me. However, it is not for me to judge the decision of another. Jesus said, *"Stop judging and you will not be judged. Stop condemning and you will not be condemned. Forgive and you will be forgiven."*[72] I must be a Cafeteria Catholic!

A cafeteria Catholic celebrates diversity in the Church. These Catholics are compassionate and respectful of doctrine. They are eager to experience Catholicism in all its nuance. A Cafeteria Catholic is a faithful Catholic.

---

[69] Boyd, Andrew "A.J". Professor of Ecumenism & Interreligious Dialogue, *If I am Catholic, but I do not agree 100% with everything that the Catholic Church teaches, does that make me no longer Catholic?* Quora Digest, Oct 2019

[70] Mission statement for Catholic Answers is a *"media ministry that serves Christ by explaining and defending the Catholic faith. We help Catholics grow in their faith, we bring former Catholics home, and we lead non-Catholics into the fullness of the truth"*.

[71] *What is a 'Cafeteria Catholic",* Catholic Answers, https://www.catholic.com/qa/what-is-a-cafeteria-catholic.

[72] Luke 6:37

Father Jack Rathschmidt, a friar for the Capuchin Franciscans Province of St. Mary, said
". . . cafeterias welcome everyone, charge very little for their food, and provide a safe
place for people to rest and [converse]. The poor, the elderly, the homeless, even large
families with small children, all know they can gather there without fear of being
evicted."[73] We would all be well served at this cafeteria.

[73] Rathschmidt, Father Jack. *Cafeteria Catholics*. Our Faith: uscatholic.org. July 29, 2008. Retrieved 8-7-2021 from: https://uscatholic.org/articles/200807/cafeteria-catholics/.

Essay 112

13 October 2022

Grace

"Amazing Grace, how sweet the sound that saved a wretch like me. I once was lost, but now am found; was blind but now I see"[74] is the opening verse of arguably the most beloved Christian hymn.

In 2015, President Obama eulogized the pastor of the Emanuel African Methodist Episcopal Church in Charleston, South Carolina. The pastor and eight parishioners were gunned down by a hate-filled terrorist during a bible study. Obama said, ". . . grace is not earned. Grace is not merited. It's not something we deserve . . ."[75] These words from a compassionate president inspired me to learn more about grace.

Then, what is grace? It is defined as a gift from God infused into the soul by the Holy Spirit to heal it of sin. That's a lot for me to process. All these years, I thought by doing good things and going to church was enough to gain favor with God.

What must I do to have grace? First, I must accept it comes from God. That's cool. Next, the Holy Spirit somehow knows I need help and keep sending it my way. I'm a little skeptical about the reasons the Spirit has chosen me, but okay, keep it coming. Third, it helps me to stop doing bad things. If it fixes my faults, I'm thankful for it. Fourth, there is nothing I can do to earn it; no good deeds will make a difference. I was hoping for the opposite, but grateful for it anyway. Lastly, I must be remorseful for my actions while being humble. Check. I can do these things.

How do I know it is working? Last week or last month or last year—doesn't matter—I would react negatively to every single thing Diane, Jack, or Bob did to rankle me. Debbie, always the family mediator, would tell me sometimes I'm stupid during these flare ups. (By the way, she's right most of the time!) Recently, I have held back my opinions and let it fester inside of me instead of being stupid. That's the Holy Spirit delivering a "size 9" to my back side!

I have never been the altar boy type. I guess the Spirit know that and has been working overtime to fix me.

Do the right thing! It has been my pursuit for a long time. If I remain true to those four words, grace will come my way.

---

[74] John Newton wrote the words to the Christian hymn "Amazing Grace" in 1772. He was an English slave trader, an Anglican minister, a hymn writer, and an abolitionist.

[75] President Obama's Eulogy to Reverend Clementa Pinckney in Charleston, SC, June 26, 2015

Essay 113

11 November 2022

"Blessed are the merciful . . ."

Thomas Aquinas stated that mercy is the "compassion in our hearts for [a] person's misery, a compassion which drives us to do what we can to help him"[76].

As Christians, we believe God sacrificed his son for our sins. Through the suffering on cross, death, and resurrection, Jesus freed man from a well-deserved punishment. It was ultimate act of mercy.

God shows mercy to those in need of help; the marginalized, the wicked, the sinful, and those suffering. He feels for us and willingly extends us a hand. God could have inflicted a harsh penalty for our actions, but offered compassion and forgiveness instead.

I believe mercy is the compassion and kindness shown to those in need of help. It is not an opportunity for me to "cherry-pick" acts of kindness to fit a narrative. It is not the giving of money or goods. It is not working a foodbank a couple of times a year. It's about shoveling my neighbor's sidewalks in the winter. It's about driving another neighbor to the doctor or grocery store.   It's about sitting on the front porch with a neighbor to pass the time.

We are a tribe of excuses. Probably the most common response when asked to extend mercy is "I would like to, but (*fill in the blank*)".

I am an excuse maker too. Sometimes I get cornered and forced to abandon my alibi and help. I usually go kicking and screaming. When the call to serve is over, a sense of satisfaction overtakes me. My reward is not a personal accomplishment, but found in the hearts of those on the receiving end.

---

[76] *Summa Theologiae* (ST II-II.30.1)

Essay 114

2 February 2023

"Blessed are the Clean of Heart"

A man goes to a grocery store with a few bucks to buy food for his family. The last few weeks have been difficult for his family. There were days with little to eat and no milk for the kids. The money in his pocket is not much, but hopes it last until the next paycheck. He had a plan for shopping; no chips or pop or sweets, just staples. After paying the cashier, he felt a sense of accomplishment. There would be enough food to last the week.

The day work he was counting on for the next week fell through. What was he going to do to make sure the kids had something to eat. With a real urgency he returned to the store. Saturdays were a busy time for the grocer. He looks for security cameras, found none, and took five cans of soup, a loaf of bread, and a gallon of milk. In a slow hurry, the man made it out of the store without being caught. He was relieved, but not feeling good. He thought, when times get better, I will make amends with the store owner.

The action of the man may be intrinsically noble, but wrong. There will be some of us that want the man put in jail. I disagree. Yes, there are foodbanks, soup kitchens, and other social services available to help, but what about the mental health of the man? Do we know anything about him or the circumstances that led to the ultimate act besides the need to feed his family? Before judging, we must understand the predicament confronting folks like him. In most cases they are destitute and fear the unknown. These emotions are intense. If we want to punish and call the man a thief, first ask is our hearts pure and without vengeance.

When we steal it is wrong. Greed, hatred, jealousy, or arrogance are also wrong and evil. There is no justification for doing a wrong. Any attempt at validation goes against human dignity and the teaching of Jesus.

The evil that troubles me the most is hate. A person can dislike another; I understand that, but to loathe so intensely that not even an ounce of empathy can be shown to someone in need is inexplicable. Why do we allow evil thoughts to consume us? I'm not sure there is a good answer to that question. I do know penetrating hatred (race, lifestyle, etc) is spreading like a California wildfire. Most of us reject this kind of hate. Regrettably, it continues to thrive in our neighborhoods and communities. Why, because we let it fester.

All of us are complicit if the hate goes without a challenge. At the top of my list of "weak-kneed" culprits are the broadcast media that call themselves journalists. When an actor makes a claim so egregious that it demands a strong rebuttal, the network goes to a commercial. By not challenging fabrications, it solicits more of the same. Where is Walter Cronkite, Dan Rather and Mike Wallace when we need them?

To rid filth from our hearts there are two approaches. One is a secular undertaking. The way forward is to acknowledge personal shortcomings and take action to neutralize these thoughts, then practice self-discipline. It is not easy to change what has been part of us for a long time. The prize awaiting us is the awareness that we have a good heart and are willing to look for the same in others.

The second approach is spiritual. We must recognize and accept the responsibility for these evils. No psychoanalyzing necessary. Simply do what Jesus tells us: *"From within people, from their hearts, come evil thoughts . . ."*[77] *"Nothing that enters one from outside can defile that person; but the things that come out from within are what defile."*[78]

A thought to contemplate: *"For where your treasure is, there also will your heart be."*[79]

---

[77] **[Mk 7:21]**
[78] **[Mk 7:15]**
[79] **[Mt 6:21]**

Essay 115

27 March 2023

"Blessed are they who hunger and thirst for righteousness"

Merriman-Webster defines righteousness as "to be morally right and justifiable". It's difficult to argue with this definition. However, M-W's interpretation implies that we in fact know right from wrong and have the tools to discern outcomes objectively . I am not convinced we have the wherewithal to do it.

Righteousness is the transformation of the heart. It is a grace from God. It is given to us by the Holy Spirit to battle the challenges in our life. This grace propels us to be humble and free of duplicity; to know virtue, morality, ethics, and honor.

James[80] in a letter to the people of Israel said: "If a brother or sister has nothing to wear and has no food for the day, and one of you says to them, 'Go in peace, keep warm, and eat well', but you do not give them the necessities of the body, what good is it?"[81]

A righteous person speaks out against injustice of any kind. Pope Francis authored a pastoral message[82] in 2018 to highlight a need to pursue justice for the disadvantaged in society. He said: "True justice comes about in people's lives when they themselves are just in their decisions . . ."

The best of us, through our actions, are righteous. They work and contribute to food banks. They help Habitat for Humanity build houses for our friends. They protect the environment every day, not just on Earth Day. They mediate disputes. They look out for their neighbors. The rest of us need to change and link arms with them to do the right thing.

Positive behavioral modification is always good, but it does not lead to rightness. We must help others for the right reasons. Acts of charity for personal aggrandizement runs counter to the teachings of Jesus. He profoundly rejected it in a parable about a Pharisee and a tax collector. He said, *"I tell you . . . for everyone who exalts himself will be humbled, and the one who humbles himself will be exalted"*.[83]

Humanitarian pursuits are only part of the challenge. We live in a toxic political environment. It has bred hatred and violence. If a solution to a problem is proposed by one side it is summarily rejected by the other. The dismissal most often is not merit-based, but directed at the source from which it comes. The polarization is tearing at the fabric of America. I's time for us to do something.

I leave you with a thought from the prophet Isaiah: "learn to do good. Make justice your aim, redress the wronged . . ."[84]

---

[80] James, likely a relative of Jesus and the leader of the Jewish Christian community in Jerusalem.

[81] **[Jas 2:15-16]**

[82] *On the Call to Holiness in Today's World*, Apostolic Exhortation, Gaudete Et Exsultate, 19 March 2018.

[83] **[Lk 18:14]**

[84] **[Is 1:17]**

Essay 116

19 May 2023

The Gifts of the Holy Spirit

In past essays, I wrote about my struggles to understand the Holy Spirit. What exactly is the role of the Spirit? I accept God as a given without feeling the need to ask why. Knowing Jesus is a palpable experience for me. We can read the Gospels and develop an opinion of him, his personality, and his role in our lives. We even know what he looks like thanks to images provided by our churches and mega movies about him. But, the Spirit? It was never that simple for me because there were no images, no warm and cozy feelings.

I eventually figured it out. Jesus was sent to us by God to teach us about right and wrong. Then, God took Jesus away to free us from all the bad things we have done. God could not allow us to meander through earthly life without someone to provide guidance. That's the Holy Spirit and how I came to accept him.

Just as I became comfortable, Christianity threw me a curveball with the gifts from the Holy Spirit. These gifts are spiritual favors. Complicating things for me was that Christians also talked about the fruit from these gifts.

I returned to the lab to learn what these gifts meant and the yield from them. I discovered the fruit is the qualities that make me a better person and the gifts are the intellectual tools necessary to produce the fruit that allows me to be that better person.

The Catholic Church promotes seven gifts of the Holy Spirit as part of its core teaching. These gifts are: wisdom, understanding, knowledge, counsel, fortitude, piety, and fear of God. The seven came from the prophet Isaiah[85]. Paul the Evangelist, in his First Letter to the Corinthians[86], listed nine gifts of the Spirit — wisdom, knowledge, faith, healing, miracles, prophecy, discerning of spirits, speaking in tongues[87], and interpretation of tongues. The list intersects, but why are they different? One explanation is the Church decided to back the prophet Isaiah over the Apostle Paul.

Confused? Here's more to chew on. The Church recognizes the fruit as: charity, joy, peace, patience, kindness, goodness, generosity, gentleness, faithfulness, modesty, self-control, and chastity. The source is Paul's letter to the Galatians (Gal 5:22-23). The passage actually lists nine. The Church added "goodness, modesty, and chastity". Why? Beats me!

For me, the easiest way to understand gifts and fruit is a tree analogy. The gifts are the roots of the tree and the fruit is the crop produced by the tree.

---

[85] **[Is 11:2-3]**

[86] **[1 Cor 12:7-11]**

[87] Speaking in "tongues" has more than a single meaning: 1) it demonstrates the ability of the Spirit to communicate; and 2) the Pentecostal view of speaking in the native language of the people.

Still confused about the gifts? The Reverend Jonathan Srock[88] helps us understand the gifts with a simple explanation. Gifts are "the ability to receive a practical answer from God to a problem you would not otherwise have discovered on your own".

The gifts are important to me, not only in a spiritual sense, but for an opportunity for discovery. To that end, I would like to discuss the gift of Fortitude and leave the others for another day.

Fortitude

Fortitude is the courage to do the right thing. It is the confidence to overcome obstacles while remaining committed to achieving a just end. Characteristics of fortitude include strength, resiliency, vigor, resolute, patience, and valor.

Today, there is a lot of noise, but little courage. Conspiracies abound in politics, healthcare, and human dignity. The debate surrounding vaccines is troubling. Science provides us with an opportunity to defeat the virus and enhance the quality life as well as life itself. Yet, the COVID-19 pandemic demonstrated how a movement with an anti-authoritarian agenda can influence the role of government in public health. It was not only the anti-vax campaigners, but attention seekers promoting conspiracy theories. It was about the dark side of humanity in search of personal gain. How many people died because of this deception? I believe these naysayers will not be judged well on the day of reckoning.

A case in point. In late 2020, front-line workers were the first to receive the COVID vaccine. A nurse at a hospital in Chattanooga was at the beginning of the line[89]. At a news conference celebrating the occasion, she fainted on the stage. The event was livestreamed on social media. What followed was a nightmare for her. Although recovery was quick, she decided to remain quiet about it. That silence launched all kind of conspiracies and outright lies about her and the vaccine. It impacted her family and friends. The cruelty was so far over the top that it was inconceivable.   The perpetrators were disgusting, pure evil.

I am proud to say that Americans (80%), in large numbers, rejected the misinformation and enthusiastically received the vaccine. The pandemic was defeated because of the fortitude of regular people to do what was right.

It seems gender identity, abortion, and racial fairness percolate to the top of mind when national elections happen in the United States. It's an indictment on the fabric of America more so than to be gay or black or to struggle with identity or to cope with an abortion decision. It also about ignorance and a failure to think. It takes an openness to explore why a teenage boy want to be a girl. It takes more than listening to the opinion of someone espousing all the sinister things that will happen when a transgender person needs to go to the bathroom. Ironically, folks claiming to be for individual liberties now insist that a person use the bathroom of their biological sex.

A person described above has a brain, a family, friends, and a heart; believe in God and country. Just like you and me. Then, why are so many enraged by the sexual orientation of another person? Answer: FEAR! People are afraid of things they don't understand. These bigots are angry and channel their

---

[88] An ordained minister in the Assemblies of God (Pentecostal denomination) and the author of the blog Divine Discourse.

[89] Source: NBC News, Brandy Zadrozny, Journalist, 10 April 2023.

petulance against anyone perceived to be a challenge to them. The most radical of them entertain violence.

The Catholic Church opposes homosexuality. This discussion is not intended to argue doctrine. It is a place to present facts. Jesus never spoke about homosexuality. We don't know his thoughts on the subject.

Paul was an important figure in the history of Christianity and known to Jesus. The Church points to the Pauline epistle to demonstrate a rejection of homosexuality. For me. it is essential we view the issue through the eyes of a compassionate Jesus. I believe he would see a LBGTQ person with the same positive attributes as any creature of God.

I never will fully be free from bias against another human being. I have evolved, but there are other days, I'm ashamed to admit, narrow-mindedness takes over. The inner voice in me screams, 'that's not you'. I know that, but it still happened and will likely happen again. Here's an incontrovertible truth about humans to burn into your brain, we are naturally prejudice organisms. Here's another, if someone needs to tell you they are not prejudice, they probably are.

Throughout my life, I have become extremely angry when someone puts down or belittles another for the way they look, act, or dress. Insensitive to the feelings of others to make yourself look superior is among the lowest forms of life. It is especially disturbing when it is directed at a child. The word that comes to mind most often to describe these people is "scum bag".

I was eight or nine years old playing a pickup game of baseball at a playground near my home that this repugnant act first reared its ugly head to me. There were two boys new to the neighborhood and recent immigrants from Italy. They spoke little English and knew less about baseball. Some kids began to make fun of them because of their differences. The teasing escalated and a fight broke out. Like most fights between kids of that age, not much came from it; some pushing with hurtful words. That is except for the younger brother.

I recall him crying uncontrollably for what was happening to his brother. So many years between then and now, but I still see that look. It was panic draped all over his face. I will never forget that experience. It made me hypersensitive to the plight of others and hostile towards the predators of the act. His name was Carman.

It's not new for kids to be cruel. It is another thing when these kids grow up and look at another person with scorn or hatred for being different. The right thing to do when someone is cruel to another is to confront it. That's not easy to do and requires guts.

Remember what Paul the Evangelist said, ". . . by the standard by which you judge another you condemn yourself."[90]

Who or what was Jim Crow?[91] The 'who' is easy, he was a character in the minstrel show of T.D. Rice—a white American stage performer in the early 1830s. He called the act "Jump, Jim Crow" and made popular the derogatory practice of blackface painting.

---

[90] **[Rom 2:1]**

[91] Article, "Who was Jim Crow?", National Geographic, *6 August 2015*

The 'what' is that Jim Crow was a harmful and demeaning representation of African Americans. It exploited speech stereotypes, movements, and physical features. To call someone Jim Crow was to point out skin color.

Jim Crow evolved into structural racism and discrimination for about a hundred years beginning in the 1870s. Jim Crow laws mandated racial segregation in all public facilities in states of the failed coup against the United States. The system established the superiority of white people in areas of intellect, morality, and civil behavior. These anti-black laws became a way of life and sanctioned racism.[92]

Jim Crow is alive and well today. Racism is part of everyday life. Good natured folks may not intend their actions or reactions to be racist, but those choices fuel racism. Here's an example of unintentional racism. Envision a discussion of Black Lives Matters with a diverse group of people. All understand the difficulty for a Black person to navigate in the racially charged environment existing today. A kind lady, part of the group, believes all people deserve equal consideration. To the group, she proclaims; "all lives matter"! The people of color, and maybe a few whites, now see her as racist. Why, because she failed to understand the inequalities existing for people of color.

Are you a racist? That's for you to decide. Knowledge and introspection will help answer that question.

Critical Race Theory (CRT) is a discipline to study how laws, the media, and movements (social and political) shape race and ethnicity perceptions. It is critical thinking. It's not about placing blame for ignorance; it is about the systematic discrimination that is entrenched in society.

Critics of CRT claim it divides people into victims of oppression and those responsible for the intolerance. These critics trace the emergence of Black Lives Matter protests and diversity training to the theory. Some went as far as blaming a program called PROMISE in Florida for the Parkland school tragedy. PROMISE provides a student guilty of a non-violent misdemeanor an opportunity to avoid school suspension/expulsion or a referral to the juvenile justice system. It's difficult to connect the dots between a program for at-risk kids and an adult with powerful weapon motivated to randomly kill other human beings.

Other critics believe CRT actually discriminate against White people. Preference in college admissions and diversity hiring practices are areas often cited as examples. Overlooked by the those opposed to admission policies of highly selective institutions is the challenges minorities experience daily to prepare for the opportunity at a chance to succeed. Whether its food insecurity, gun violence, or inferior K-12 schools, these kids looking to be educated at the best colleges deserve a little extra consideration. Not anymore.

The Supreme Court struck down admission policies at two highly selective universities effectively ending affirmative action. The noble goal of many colleges and universities to create a diverse student body for the greater good has been made more difficult. The irony of the decision is that affirmative action in its totality was not banned for admission consideration. WHAT? If an applicant is considered a "legacy"[93] candidate or an athletic recruit or an early admit does not fall under the Supreme Court ruling.

---

[92] Jim Crow Museum, Ferris State University, Big Rapids, Michigan

[93] Legacy admission (legacy preference) to a college refers to a policy of giving special consideration to a prospective student because the applicant is related to an alumnus or a donor.

As reported in Rolling Stone, Michelle Obama said of the Supreme Court decision: "So often, we just accept that money, power, and privilege are perfectly justifiable forms of affirmative action, while kids growing up like I did are expected to compete when the ground is anything but level."[94] A powerful statement and true.

CRT has become a lightning rod for right-wing zealots and most conservative politicians. By the way, clandestine and open racists are energized by it. What should be about understanding differences and working to achieve the good has provided a forum for White Rage.

What is White Rage? It is the systematic oppression of opportunity for Black people. It is white supremacy and rooted in a fear of altering the current power dynamics. White people believe the privileges that come with being white is threatened by black equality and opportunity. Additionally, it is embedded in the legal system; in institutions, with government officials, and in law enforcement. White Rage is central to understanding extreme-right racists. They are convinced the White race is under siege and to salvage it, violence is appropriate against the perpetrator.

Don't be fooled by the critics of CRT. It not about remembering an uncomfortable history, it is about restoring Jim Crow to American society. Remember what Jesus said, *"Beware of false prophets, who come to you in sheep's clothing, but underneath are ravenous wolves."* [95]

Concerned people should be alarmed with the direction of local school boards. There is a movement to ban books deemed unacceptable. These efforts are designed to prevent educators in public schools from presenting an unvarnished examination of American history and civics. It is a blatant attempt at restricting free speech.

The proponents of the ban want us to believe it is about education and morality. NO! It is about grievance. NO! It's about frustration with social and economic standing. YES, it's about race and identity.[96]

The mood in the United States remains noxious. It has been that way for a while. When a cop steps on the throat of a Black man, protests breakout all over. Racist blame the dead guy for escalating the situation. Maybe it time for the deniers to look in the mirror and "man up".

Abortion is wrong. It is not a decision for others to make. By "others" I mean not me or you or groups or governments or churches. It is a life altering decision, and for that reason, belongs to the woman. She bears the consequences for it, good or bad.

Here's something to ponder. A man committed a sin of lust. We learned he is devoutly religious and recalled that Jesus said, *"if your right hand causes you to sin, cut it off and throw it away. It is better for you to lose one of your members than to have your whole body go into Gehenna."*[97] He atoned for his imprudence by cutting off his hand!

There are no laws that address this type of bodily mutilation or adultery in the United States. The only sanction he received is to live with the decision. The point here is that there are good and bad laws.

---

[94] Bort, Ryan. "Michelle Obama Sounds Off on Affirmative Action Decision: 'My Heart Breaks'", Rolling Stone Magazine, 29 June 2023.

[95] **[Mt 7:15]**

[96] PEN America reported that book banning "continue to target stories by and about people of color and LGBTQ+ individuals." In first half of the 2022-23 school year, 30% of the banned books are about race, racism, or feature characters of color. Meanwhile, 26% have LGBTQ+ characters or themes."

[97] **[Mt 5:28,30]**

Legislating against a right of a person to make a decision about their body belongs to them and not governments.

Do you remember when our legislators were highly principled with integrity? I do. Let me qualify that by saying at least most politicians had values and worked in the best interest of the country. Today, there are some that remain guided by principle, but money and power rules the day now.

John F. Kennedy wrote a book about the human virtue of valor. Profiles in Courage[98] detailed the careers of eight United States senators for demonstrating fortitude under enormous political pressure to do otherwise. The bravery of these senators changed their political trajectory and most lost reelections.

Courage as defined by President Kennedy: "In whatever arena of life, one may meet the challenge of courage, whatever may be the sacrifices he faces if he follows his conscience—the loss of his friends, his fortune, his contentment, even the esteem of his fellow men—each man must decide for himself the course he will follow. The stories of past courage can define that ingredient—they can teach, they can offer hope, they can provide inspiration. But they cannot supply courage itself. For this each man must look into his own soul."[99]

---

[98] *Profiles in Courage*, John F. Kennedy, Harper & Brothers, New York, 1956
[99] Ibid.

Essay 117

19 August 2023

Beatitudes

What are the Beatitudes? In the simplest of terms, Beatitudes are a roadmap for living a good life. These blessings from Jesus show us how to be a better person while contributing to humanity in a positive way.

There are two competing translations of the Beatitudes. In the "Sermon on the Mount", Mathew underscored the faith and spiritual values taught by Jesus. Luke's version, called the "Sermon on the Plain", emphasized social wellness. There are intersections for sure; however, the different approaches allow for thoughtful discussion.

Another consideration for the divergence was the audiences of the authors. Mathew's mission was to convince Jewish Christians of the importance of Jesus as a teacher eclipsing the reputation of Moses. If you need to rank things, Moses delivered the oppressed to the "promise land"; Jesus promised to deliver us to the Kingdom of Heaven. Mathew's blessings focused primarily on that journey. Luke tailored his message to a Gentile Christian audience by addressing economic and social conditions.

The Beatitudes require contemplation. These blessings were not always intended to be taken literally. Instead, Jesus wants us to think and reflect on their meaning in a deep and deliberative way. In other words, make it personal. That is my intent with this discussion.

A little housekeeping before exploring the Beatitudes. As noted previously, the Gospels of Matthew and Luke had similar reporting of the message from Jesus. For brevity purpose, I chose to merge these versions. As in other essays, I write from a personal perspective.

Beatitude #1:
"Blessed are the poor in spirit, for theirs is the kingdom of heaven (Matthew 5:3).
> To be "poor in spirit" brings up a contradiction of sorts for me. Society thinks being poor is an economic anomaly not a crisis. Food insecurity, violence, injustice are associated with the struggles of the poor; that's a definition of a crisis.
>
> Many believe the disadvantaged are without hope. That's a convenient way for people with means to avoid getting involved or helping. The difference between the haves and have nots is that people with resources see tomorrow as a day of opportunity not despair. It's naive for anyone not to recognize the poor desperately want and need to be optimistic.
>
> Many of the poor feel abandon by God due to the challenges of earthly life. Feeling unwanted by society makes it difficult to trust when the focus is on the next meal or a place to sleep for the night. The poor do not want to be faithless, but repeated knock downs make it difficult to believe God will be there for them.

"Blessed are you who are poor, for the kingdom of God is yours" (Luke 6:20).
> Luke's Gospel demonstrates a special concern for the disenfranchised in society. Is it because Luke was a Gentile? Likely. He was also a physician, a historian, and a devout follower of Saint

Paul the Evangelist. His Gospel is considered by biblical scholars as the most accurate historical representation of the life of Jesus and the emergence of Christian evangelism.

Luke, more than any other Gospel authors, wrote frequently about the social and economic impact on people. There is little doubt he was influenced by the compassion of Jesus for the poor, the oppressed, and the least of God's creatures. Luke championed the economically distressed in society with little or no money, food insecurity, mounting debt, injustice, and easily extorted by wretched prey. He would be called a social activist today.

"But woe to you who are rich, for you have received your consolation" (Luke 6:24).
On any context, "to woe" is not something I look forward to be said about me. It is a warning of
Luke tells the wealthy to enjoy life now for that's the best it is going to get for them.

In any context, "to woe" is not something I look forward to be said about me. It is a warning of impending doom. When Luke used it to make a statement about the conduct of wealthy people, it is time for soul-searching.

Pope Francis said: "We cannot wait for the poor to knock on our door; we need urgently to reach them in their homes, in hospitals and nursing homes, on the streets and in the dark corners where they sometimes hide, in shelters and reception centers."[100]

The message from the Holy Father is akin to the pregame speech[101] by Herb Brooks, coach of the 1980 United States Winter Olympics hockey team. The American team was to play the Soviet Union for the gold medal. The Soviets were the greatest hockey team in the world. Coach Brooks said, *"if we* played them ten times, they might win nine. But not this game, not tonight. Tonight, we are the greatest hockey team in the world. This is your time. Now go out there and take it!" The team burst through the locker room door and on to the ice. One of the players stopped short of the rink, turned to a teammate, and with a look of bewilderment, asked "how do we do it"?

How do we do help the least of us? First, we must recognize the economic hardship and social standing of poor people. It's more than the next meal or a place to sleep for the night. It's about surviving for the next hour.

Trust is essential. If a person cannot trust the messenger, how can disadvantaged people begin to recover. A long time ago, I asked a business supplier what is the most important quality in developing a relationship with a customer. I expected a response like an exceptional product or superior customer service. He responded—"make a friend". That is excellent advice for building trust.

Beatitude #2
"Blessed are the meek, for they will inherit the land" (Matthew 5:4).
On 30 June, I wrote about this Beatitude in Essay #101: *"The Meek Shall Come to Rule the World"*.

---

[100] Message of His Holiness Pope Francis for the Fifth World Day of the Poor, 14 November 2021

[101] Note: The original speech was done in a private locker room; Kurt Russell recreated the speech in the film "Miracle" (O'Connor, Gavin. 2004. Miracle. United States: Buena Vista Pictures).

Beatitude #3

"Blessed are they who mourn, for they will be comforted" (Matthew 5:5).

We mourn for many reasons. The death of someone near to us or a serious illness of a family member or the concern we have for a friend challenged with a life-altering event are examples of grief.

Other forms of mourning are more personal. How about when we do harm, by accident or intent, resulting in great anguish to someone? A remorseful person suffers. It's not easy to overcome the hurt we feel. Most of us would like to go back and have a do over.

Another example of mourning is the fear felt by someone of regressing to their former self. It is difficult to avoid the traps that got us there in the first place. In the parable of the lost sheep: Jesus said, *"I tell you, in just the same way there will be more joy in heaven over one sinner who repents than over ninety-nine righteous people who have no need of repentance."*[102]

"Blessed are you who are now weeping, for you will laugh" (Luke 6:21).

An emotion that solicits tears comes from the heart. Tears of happiness for someone are genuine. At the other boundary are cries for help.

During a pastoral visit to the Philippines in 2015[103], Pope Francis met a weeping 12-year-old Filipino girl. She was abandoned and forced to rummage through garbage for food. She slept in the open without shelter from the elements. Her name is Glyzelle Palomar. She asked Francis a question: "Why did God let this happen to us?" Francis was emotionally moved by the little girl and her question. He did not have an answer. Some were surprised that he did not. But the gift of the Holy Father is his pastor's heart—he is honest and authentic. Rarely does the spiritual, or for that matter, the secular community have answers to complex problem of world suffering.

After Francis's encounter with Glyzelle, he scraped his prepared remarks and spoke off the cuff. From the beginning of his leadership of the Church, Francis was known for his humanity. With that quality, it is easy to understand the empathy he showed for the little girl. He talked about tears, suffering, and despair.

"If you laugh, think and cry, that's a heck of a day."[104] Jim Valvano, a college basketball coach, spoke these words two months before he died of cancer. To cry followed by laughter is more than a day's work. It is the fulfilment of a life.

Beatitude #4

"Blessed are they who hunger and thirst for righteousness, for they will be satisfied" (Matthew 5:6).

Righteousness defined is "to be morally right and justifiable".[105] It's difficult to argue with this definition. Another way to define it is to be right in the eyes of God. A third interpretation is to

---

[102] **[Lk 15:4–7]**

[103] Source: National Catholic Reporter, *"Francis struggles to answer crying girl's question about suffering"* by Joshua J. McElwe, 18 January 2015.

[104] Jim Valvano, 1993 ESPY Awards

[105] Merriam-Webster.com Dictionary, s.v. "righteous," accessed June 18, 2024, https://www.merriam-webster.com/dictionary/righteous.

do the right thing! Common to all implies that we in fact know right from wrong. I'm not convinced we do.

Jesus made it easy for us. By allowing his crucifixion, our sins were pardoned and we became righteous. Over time, we squandered that gift. Now, we need to do the work to regain it. I can't imagine what it would be like to be righteous all the time.

"Blessed are you who are now hungry, for you will be satisfied. . ." (Luke 6:21).
It is our responsibility to strive to eradicate food insecurity for all people. That is a goal for good-intended people with a quixotic view of world hunger. The realty of the problem is that not enough of us care about solving it. If we did, there would not be agencies like Feed the Hungry[106] soliciting help to provide the necessary sustenance for people around the world. There would not be a need for Feeding America[107] or Meals on Wheels[108].

Luke is smiling for the work of these advocates. At the same time, he would ask why can't we figure out a better way to solve hunger.

"But woe to you who are filled now, for you will be hungry. . ." (Luke 6:25).
Hunger, like protecting earthly resources, lack a commitment to do something about it. The dark side of humanity reveals that a problem needs to affect us in a personal way before a willingness to act becomes urgent. Climate change is an example. For the most part, it is a threat that too many global citizens reject. That is, until the sea level rise in places like Miami Beach and we move about in row boats. Wait, the folks in South Dakota are unfazed by the hardship of Floridians? South Dakotans and like-minded people are all about "what's in it for me" before they are willing to help.

Beatitude #5
"Blessed are the merciful, for they will be shown mercy" (Matthew 5:7).
On 21 July, I wrote about this Beatitude in Essay #113: *"Blessed are the merciful . . ."*.

Beatitude #6
"Blessed are the clean of heart, for they will see God" (Matthew 5:8).
On 19 May, I wrote about this Beatitude in Essay #114: *""Blessed are the Clean of Heart"*.

Beatitude #7
"Blessed are the peacemakers, for they will be called children of God" (Matthew 5:9).
On 10 March, I wrote about this Beatitude in Essay #128: *"Blessed are the peacemakers, for they will be called children of God."*

Beatitude #8
"Blessed are they who are persecuted for the sake of righteousness, for theirs is the kingdom of heaven" (Matthew 5:10).
Most of the time, defining a subject helps me develop an approach to understand it. Dictionary.com defines persecuting as "to pursue with harassing or oppressive treatment,

---

[106] Feed the Hungry is a faith-based charity dedicated to feeding the poor and hungry.

[107] Feeding America provides food to people through a nationwide network of food banks, food pantries, and meal programs.

[108] Meals on Wheels is a community-based program dedicated to addressing senior isolation and hunger.

especially because of religious or political beliefs, ethnic or racial origin, gender identity, or sexual orientation".

Systematic racism thought to be on its way to extinction during the civil rights movement in the 1960s, continues to expose the ugly side of humanity today. For many years, discrimination was subtly injected into society. Country clubs, gated communities, and healthcare are examples. Now, racists go in front of the camera and proclaim they reject it in any form, but support restrictions on the rights of minorities to vote.

"Blessed are you when people hate you, and when they exclude and insult you, and denounce your name as evil on account of the Son of Man" (Luke 6:22).
> We must speak out against injustice in any form. Pope Francis said: "True justice comes about in people's lives when they themselves are just in their decisions; it is expressed in their pursuit of justice for the poor and the weak . . ." [109]

A final thought; Isiah said: ". . . learn to do good. Make justice your aim . . ."[110]

---

[109] Pope Francis, para 79, "Rejoice and be Glad (Gaudete et Exsultate)", Apostolic Exhortation, 19 March 2018.
[110] **[Is] 1:17]**

Essay 118

21 October 2023

Vile Words

Approaching this topic, my initial inclination was to title it "Bad Words". If you are like me, the first thing that came to mind with that label was cussing. "Vile Words" is more what I intend to discuss.

Some words erode self-confidence while others demonstrate ignorance. Still others, like racial slurs or ethnic inferences confirm a deep-seated prejudice against people that are different. It is discrimination, plain and simple. "It's not my fault that my job doesn't pay me enough. If I was a black man, I would be the boss." Or, "that kid got my scholarship because she is poor". Missing in these examples is promotions and scholarships are earned, not an entitlement.

Discrimination is not new. Derogatory words are not new. These forms of "vile words" have existed for a long time, too long. What is all too apparent to me is that many of us speak callously about others without a nano second of thought of the impact on the them.

I remember playing tag as a child with a bunch of neighborhood friends. It began with the chanting of a rhyme.

Eenie, meenie, miney, moe,
Catch a tiger by the toe,
If he hollers, let him go,
Eenie, meenie, miney, moe

The first kid was "eenie"; the second was "meenie" and so on until someone became "moe". The unlucky kid that was "moe"—he or she—was "it" and forced to chase the others to try to tag them.

Many call it a counting game. But I recall another version of the rhyme. The word "tiger" was replaced with "n!@@&r". That was in the late 1950s and early 1960s. All these years have passed and I still don't know why we choose that word. Most of us were not racially prejudice or even aware that maybe our parents held private thoughts against "colored" people. I do know this; the group of kids were all white.

In the world today, we are forced to choose our words carefully to avoid being called a homophobe or racist. Here's a reality check; if that is why you do it, then you are probably one of them. Here's another flash for you; the loudest voices in opposition to sensitivity are racists and intolerants.

To that end, I would like to list some pejorative words and expressions that are cruel and ignorant.

AC/DC—angry white man—Aunt Jamima—bimbo—bitch—camel jockey—
chick-with-a-d@!k—Coon—cracker—cougar—cunt—dick, dyke—faggot—
fairy—homo—gold-digger—gook—hunky—hymie—honky—Jim Crow—
jungle bunny—Karen—Macaca—mick—MILF—nigger—niggeritis—oreo—
prick—queer—raghead—Redskin—slut—spearchucker—spook—spaz—
Spic—switch-hitter—tranny—Uncle Tom—white trash—welfare queen—
wigger—wop

What are you thinking after reading these words? Are you appalled by the cruelty? You should be. They are mean and degrading things to say to anyone. They hurt and undermine a person's self-confidence, a feeling of belonging, and happiness.

Mean words or phrases is bullying, PERIOD! For a bully to feel good about himself the target must feel bad. The problem for the bully is the euphoria with perceived dominance only last for a short time. They need to do it again and again. That's a sad commentary about someone. Eventually, the bully runs out of targets. Then, what is that person to do? Frankly, I don't care.

Targets of bullies lose self-esteem and the confidence to do great things. It's time we pump up the targets and find help for the bullies. Here's a few examples of hurtful idioms that disparages someone self-worth.

"You're stupid".
"You're f#!%!&g stupid".
"You are so fat".
"You're ugly."
"You're worthless."

I would like to close with a real story about ethnic insensitivity. Debbie and I witnessed it on a trip to Greece several years ago. For those of you that have not been to the Greek Isles, there are many opportunities to buy things from small shops and street vendors. During one of the stops, a lady, asked another couple if they were able to "Jew down" the seller? We have heard that expression many times in our lifetime. The problem this time, the other couple was Jewish. The lady was truly remorseful; I don't doubt that for a minute. Although I haven't seen that lady in more than twenty years, I believe the incident still percolates up as an uncomfortable memory.

The intent of the essay is to acknowledge people make mistakes and the good ones regret it. They learn from their insensitivity. Our challenge going forward is to help the people that intentionally utter vile words. We can call them out or embarrass the perpetrator, whatever works, but change them.

Essay 119

Unforgivable Sin

I was surprised to learn there is something called an "unforgivable sin". I understand there are some things that are bad and some things not so bad. The Catholic Church calls the bad things grave sins and the not so bad venial sins; but "unforgiveable"!

I believe that all sins may be forgiven as long as the sinner is truly contrite and reconciles the act with God. It took me a long time to understand how a murderer can be excused for taking the life of someone. If I want to walk with Jesus, then I must accept pardoning an actor guilty of the most egregious act.

Before getting to what is an unforgivable sin, I would like to discuss what the Catholic Church says about sin along with how Jesus interprets the commandments.

What is a sin? Do we really understand sinfulness? How do we come to commit a sin? What does Jesus call a sin? A good place to begin is the Catechism of the Catholic Church. The Church defines a sin as an offense against "reason, truth, and right conscience".[111]

In Judaism and because of the Mosaic Covenant[112] came the law of Moses—all 613 of them. Included in the list are the Ten Commandments; the guide to living a righteous life. According to Chapter 19 in the Book of Exodus, punishment for breaking one of the laws calls for a harsh consequence. If you are inclined, follow the link[113] in the footnote for a complete list of Mosaic law. By the way, I made it through about 50 laws before becoming bored.

A note from Paul the Evangelist about the law of Moses: in a letter to the Galatians, he claimed it was okay to ignore Mosaic law (Galatians 5:18) if the Holy Spirit is our guide. I imagine that statement created a near cataclysmic event in the early Church and among Jews. It was heresy, they said of Paul's assertion! Wrong. Paul believed in the holy Trinity – the Father, Son, and Holy Spirit. His intent was to allow the Spirit to lead us towards the proper end.

Back to the discussion to what is a sin or, as Moses called it, a punishment. Let's begin with the Ten Commandments. It's obvious to most Christians, a violation of a commandment is a serious departure from rightness. Is that the beginning and end of it? Saint Paul thinks not. He said to the Galatians that sin is "works of the flesh" and listed immorality, impurity, waste, hatred, jealousy, selfishness, envy, among others.[114] Paul's list is exhaustive and covers about everything a human could do wrong. Our challenge is to understand the severity of a sinful act. Is it an offense against God or a failure of humanism?

---

[111] (CCC 1849)

[112] A contract between the Israelites and God as revealed by Moses.

[113] https://www.chabad.org/library/article_cdo/aid/756399/jewish/The-613-Commandments-Mitzvot.htm

[114] **[Gal 5:19-21]**

Sins are evaluated according to their gravity. The two types are called mortal and venial. A mortal sin is the intentional turning away from God. It is a violation of the Ten Commandments. There are three conditions necessary for a sin to be mortal. First, the act is consequential. Second, it is known to be wrong. Third, it is deliberate and made freely by us.

A venial sin is a less serious infraction and does not break the covenant with God. With God's grace it is reparable; however, it does require remedial action. Catholics call it temporal punishment. The sacrament of Reconciliation is necessary to expunge the sin. If the Penance is not carried out, then it remains with the sinner.

An analogy to explain temporal punishment is during a pickup baseball game, a batted ball breaks a window in the house next door. The batter apologizes to the neighbor and it is accepted. But the window is still broken and needs fixed. The broken window is the temporal consequence and the fixing of it is the discharging of the mistake.

What did Jesus think about the Commandments? In the Gospel of Mark[115], as Jesus began his journey from Galilee to Jerusalem, a rich man approached him with a question about living forever. Jesus responded with, *"you know the commandments: 'You shall not kill; you shall not commit adultery; you shall not steal; you shall not bear false witness; you shall not defraud; honor your father and your mother.'"* The man affirmed his compliance. Next, Jesus said, *"You are lacking in one thing. Go, sell what you have, and give to [the] poor and you will have treasure in heaven; then come, follow me."* With that condition the rich man, dejected and disappointed, departed from Jesus.

The significance of the story was not the plea of the man, but the commandments Jesus identified as essential to be admitted to Heaven. Surprisingly, he excluded five of the Ten Commandments recognized by Judaism and Christianity; and similar in Islam. Some of these omitted commandments are considered the bedrock of Mosaic law. Moreover, Jesus added *"You shall not defraud"* to the list.

The addition of *"You shall not defraud"* aligns with my earthly values. By my standard, the lack of empathy for the underserved in society is a mortal sin. My neighbors and government sometimes fail to see it as I do. It seems more important to these people to restrict a person right of self-determination through legislation than to grab the hand of a homeless man and help him take the first step on the road to societal integration.

The part of the Ten Commandments Jesus chose to highlight focused on ethical and social behaviors. Those omitted included the worship of false gods; the singularity of one God; honoring God by not slandering His name; and respecting the Sabbath. Also, absent is the commandments concerning "to covet". As extraordinary as the omission of service to God, Jesus chose to add a strong statement of personal responsibility — *"you shall not defraud"* the less fortunate.

Jesus was asked what was the most important commandment. He replied, *"The first is this: 'Hear, O Israel! The Lord our God is Lord alone!"*[116] In the mind of Jesus and every Jew, Muslim, and Christian, monotheism[117] is a given. The reason Jesus did not include the commandment with his list is because it should be self-evident to all Christians.

---

[115] [Mk 10:17-31]

[116] [Mk 12:29]

[117] Monotheism: the doctrine or belief that there is but one God .Merriam-Webster.com Dictionary, s.v. "monotheism," accessed December 4,

The absence of the commandment about taking the Lord's name in vain is perplexing to me. There is no reference (evidence) Jesus expected us to revere the Lord and not misuse His name. In Luke 6:46, Jesus asserts: *"Why do you call me, 'Lord, Lord', but not do what I command?"* That declaration strongly suggest Jesus views the commandment prominently.

Reserving a day for reflection depends on the religion. The Muslim sabbath is Friday, the Jewish sabbath is from sunset Friday and ends at dark on Saturday, and the Christian sabbath is Sunday. Exodus 20:8 states: "Six days you may labor and do all your work, but the seventh day is a sabbath of the LORD your God." We interpret this verse as defining a work week as Monday through Friday, and maybe Saturday. What about a steelworker working a 20-turn schedule? The point is not setting aside a day for the sabbath or how many days someone works, it is about finding time to walk with Jesus to make us better humans.

Did Jesus mean by excluding "to covet another's wife" from his list that it is not a sin; or should it be considered adultery? The desire to "hit on" the wife of your neighbor is the prelude to having a sexual encounter with that person. If that happens, it is considered adultery; if it doesn't, then what is it? E. Bruce Brooks of the Warring States Project at the University of Massachusetts Amherst wrote: "Merely coveting a neighbor's wife is not a sin; only the act of adultery would be a sin."[118] I believe tracking someone like a neighbor's wife is a temptation or intention without action. it is not a violation of a commandment. Is it wrong? Of course.

"To covet" the possessions of others fit comfortably with the commandments to not steal or lie. If we are willing to steal from someone, we are likely to make a false acquisition against that same person.

With my personal observations of the excluded commandments over, let's review the commandments Jesus endorsed in story of the rich man found in the Gospel of Mark.

The Commandments of Jesus
"Honor your father and your mother."
This commandment is about respect and responsibility for others. Respect is a virtue. Why is it considered that? As defined by the Markkula Center at Santa Clara University, respect is an attitude or disposition or character trait necessary to achieve ethical principles.[119] Other virtues are honesty, courage, compassion, generosity, fidelity, integrity, and fairness.

A child comes into the world honoring their mother and father. It's up to the parents to put in the work necessary to nurture that relationship. To strengthen a parent-child partnership, dialogue leads to the discovery of a common purpose. Sustaining an unbroken line of communication will yield dividends.

Some interpret "honor" to mean "obey". It is not. Merriman-Webster defines honor "to regard or treat (someone) with admiration and respect." To obey is "to comply with or follow the commands, restrictions, wishes, or instructions" of another.[120] When we hear the word "obey" many emotions surface; some good, others not so good. Traffic laws are created for the greater good. They should be

---

2023, https://www.merriam-webster.com/dictionary/monotheism.

[118] E Bruce Brooks, Jesus and After: The First Eighty Years, Studies in Early Christianity, Warring States Project, 2017.

[119] Velasquez, Andre, Shanks, Meyer, Article, *Issues in Ethics* V1 N3 (1988), Markkula Center, Santa Clara University.

[120] Dictionary.com

adhered to accept the consequences for violating them. Forced to obey a controversial command has the potential to be overwhelming. To submit to a directive that is divisive at its core never achieves the desired outcome.

"You shall not kill."
A better translation from Hebrew would be "thou shalt not murder"; a subtle distinction but an important one to the Christians. Killing an innocent person is considered murder. Killing an unjust aggressor to preserve your own life is still killing, but it not considered murder.

"You shall not commit adultery."
The Catechism of the Catholic Church defines adultery as "marital infidelity".[121] When two consenting parties (at least one is married) have sexual relations it is adultery. Additionally, the Catechism defines fornication as a "carnal union between an unmarried man and an unmarried woman."[122] How is a "carnal union" different from adultery; is it the same as fornication or carnal knowledge or intercourse? I looked it up. The answer is YES.

Anyone violating this commandment made a huge blunder. It should not be a "death sentence" for the wrongdoer.   The Church provides a way to earn forgiveness. That's not enough for me. We must atone for the mistake by following the moral code of Jesus. If the opportunity for another adulterous relationship presents itself, the forgiven adulterer must steadfastly reject the temptation to do it again.

There will be those that say repeat violators of a grave sin does not deserve absolution for the act. I disagree. First, the actor is remorseful and truly believes it will never happen again. These are conditions for forgiveness and the granting of absolution. Second, regardless of the number of times the sin is repeated, the sinner will eventually get it and begin to live a life in keeping with God's intent for us. Isn't that why God forgives us?

"You shall not steal."
What it means to steal should be apparent to all. Not so apparent is that stealing can be taking advantage of a person. It could be economic theft or exploitation of someone for profit; robbing the victim of dignity; or to take something that belongs to another.

"You shall not bear false witness against your neighbor."
This commandment is an offense against the truth. It's lying! It is intentional and meant to deceive.

"You shall not defraud [the less fortunate]."
The intention of Jesus by including "defraud" is exemplified by words attributed to Moses in Deuteronomy: "You shall not exploit a poor and needy hired servant . . . each day you shall pay the servant's wages before the sun goes down . . . Otherwise, the servant will cry to the LORD against you, and you will be held guilty."[123]

Understanding wealth during the times of Jesus is essential to appreciate the inclusion of this commandment. A wealthy landowner most likely owned many farms. These landowners relied on tenant farmers to work the fields. The accumulation of the landowner's wealth came at the expense of the worker. Amassing wealth would have been unlikely without cheating hired hands.

---

[121] (CCC 2380)

[122] (CCC 2353)

[123] **[Deut 24:14–15]**

Earlier in this essay, I wrote of an encounter between Jesus and a rich man. Remember what he said to the man: "*. . . sell what you have, and give to [the] poor and you will have treasure in heaven .*" Jesus then asked his disciples a question, "*How hard it is for those who have wealth to enter the kingdom of God?*" He didn't wait for their answer and said, "*It is easier for a camel to pass through [the] eye of [a] needle than for one who is rich to enter the kingdom of God.*"[124]

This new commandment seeks economic justice for the less fortunate among us. More generally, it asks us to be an advocate for all forms of injustice. The prophet Micah said: "You have been told, O mortal, what is good, and what the LORD requires of you: Only to do justice and to love goodness, and to walk humbly with your God."[125]

The Omitted Commandments

As noted earlier, I was puzzled by the exclusion of the commandment dealing with the misuse of the Lord's name. Although, the reasoning presented for excluding the allegiance to one God seems solid, if I compiled a list of commandments, these two would make the cut. To that end, I am including a discussion on them.

"I am the LORD your God. You shall worship the Lord your God and Him only shall you serve."
The commandment forbids idolatry and the worship of false gods. When Jesus was asked by a scribe to choose the greatest commandment, he said, "*You shall love the Lord, your God, with all your heart, with all your soul, and with all your mind.*"[126]

"You shall not take the name of the Lord your God in vain."
When I think of taking God's name in vain, the first thing that come to mind is using it in anger. JESUS CHRIST!!! Any time I have used it to express an emotion, it makes me angry. Why couldn't I find a better word to express my displeasure? I know it was not out of disrespect for Jesus, but it passed through my lips so easily.

Kevin Considine, in an article for U.S. Catholic, stated the commandment has little to do with a moment of verbal declaration. "Rather, it is a warning about putting God's name and approval on anything violent or harmful to our fellow creatures."[127]

We tend to cavalierly proclaim an oath with God's name attached to it; "so help me God" or "I swear to God" to affirm a truth without understanding the consequences of swearing to it falsely.

The Crusades are an example of using God's name to justify an action. There were eight major expeditions in all and occurred during the High Middle Ages (circa 1000 to 1300 CE). The Crusades were religious wars between Christians and Muslims to secure control of land sacred to both groups. The Crusades made it easy to justify actions by invoking God's will.

What is the unforgiveable sin?

---

[124] [Mk 10:21,23,25]
[125] [Micah 6:8]
[126] [Mt 22:38]
[127] Considine, Kevin, "What does it mean to take God's name in vain?", U.S. Catholic, *2023 Vol. 88, No. 9, p. 49.*

Jesus said: "*Amen, I say to you, all sins and all blasphemies that people utter will be forgiven them. But whoever blasphemes against the holy Spirit will never have forgiveness . . .*"[128]

The apostle John called blasphemy against the Holy Spirit a "conscious rejection of the truth".[129]

Kenneth Berding, a blogger, said: "Blasphemy against the Spirit—the unforgivable sin—is *ongoing hardening of your heart* against the Holy Spirit . . ."[130]

For those of us not sure what it means to be blasphemous here's a secular definition of the term along with an explanation from Pope John Paul II. According to the Merriam-Webster dictionary, it is "the act of insulting or showing contempt or lack of reverence for God."[131] The Pope took a slightly different approach in defining it. He stated, "Blasphemy . . . [is] the refusal to accept the salvation which God offers to man through the Holy Spirit . . ."[132]

A final thought from Rick Phillips of the Tenth Presbyterian Church in Philadelphia: ". . . let me assure you that if you are worried that you may have committed the unforgivable sin that is strong testimony that you have not; if your heart were hardened enough to commit the sin you would no longer be concerned about your eternal state . . . If you believe and confess in your heart that Jesus is Lord and Savior, then you have *accepted* the Spirit's testimony and by definition have not blasphemed against it."[133]

---

[128] [Mk 3:28-29]
[129] [1 John 5:6]
[130] Berding, Kenneth. Blog: "What is the Unforgiveable Sin?", Biola University, 3 Feb 2021.
[131] Merriam-Webster.com Dictionary, *s.v.* "blasphemy," accessed September 28, 2023.
[132] John Paul II, General Audience, Wednesday, 24 May 1989
[133] Phillips, Rick. Article: "What Is Blasphemy against the Holy Spirit?', Tenth Presbyterian Church, 23June 2002.

Essay 120

29 November 2023

Crisis with the Church not Faith

As I began preparing for this essay, my mindset was to examine what it meant to be at a crossroads spiritually. The dilmena for me was to understand what it meant to be faithless. Is it nihilism? If true, then the challenger must be an atheist or tending in that direction. I came up with nothing worthy of a hypothesis to explore. In the end, there is no crisis with my faith. I never questioned my belief in God, Jesus, or Sacred Scripture. With that said, I really don't understand how someone could come to a disconnect with God. On the other hand, it is crystal clear to me how someone can be disillusioned with the Catholic Church. I call it a "crisis with the Church". Before exploring how people like me have a problem with the Church in America, I would like to look at what is faith.

What is faith? I can only speak about the meaning of faith to me. I know from the Book of Genesis, "God created mankind in his image; in the image of God, he created them; male and female he created them."[134] Moses is credited with writing the book along with the books of Exodus, Leviticus, Numbers, and Deuteronomy. Scholars claim these books were written during the 5th and 6th centuries BCE. If so, Moses would have been several hundred years old. Authorship of the first five books of the Bible is inconsequential. What is important to me is that I may resemble God.

In another reference to what God looks like, Paul wrote to the Colossians, "[Jesus] is the image of the invisible God . . ."[135] That's enough for me to accept the existence of God.

The next step is to believe God is the reason I eat, walk, think, breath, and more. It may surprise some, but I do believe that.

Pope Francis said this about it; "Having faith means keeping your heart turned to God . . ." The Bishop of Rome also said "Faith makes us walk with Jesus on the roads of this world . . ."

In the letter to the Hebrews (Chap 11), faith is described as "the realization of what is hoped for and evidence of things not seen. . . By faith we understand that the universe was ordered by the word of God, so that what is visible came into being through the invisible . . . for anyone who approaches God must believe that he exists . . ."[136]

A person in a spiritual crisis question everything that was celebrated as truth. Is God real? Is God good? Is it worth putting trust in God? Another question deserving an answer, did this person ever have faith in God in the first place?

---

[134] [Gn 1:27]

[135] [Col 1:15]

[136] [Heb 11:1,3,6]

As noted earlier, my faith in God is not in crisis. I do not question the revealed truths from Sacred Scripture or Apostolic Tradition[137]. How could I doubt my faith? These truths come from Jesus or witnessed by his disciples. When the Church teaches about these truths, Catholics listen.

My crisis is with the Church when it veers into the social and political arenas.

What is a crisis with the Church? The Mass is more entertaining in recent years. There is more singing compared to a time when there was none. Homily are better, but many priests still read from a prepared text much like that boring professor many of us were forced to endure. Ministries have become the axis to encourage involvement in parish life beyond the hour each week in church. There seems to be a genuine attempt to connect with members. This new approach begs a question, is the change intended to appease those attending Mass or is it to encourage the wayward parishioners to reconnect with the Church? I don't know the answer. What I do know is that cosmetic changes will not make anyone more Catholic.

Just as we begin to think the Church has changed to be more accommodating, the ugly head of influence robs our hope. In another essay I revealed the one hour a week at Mass is for me to become more like Jesus. Instead, the Church lectures me about the evils of the right to self-determination and how I must think and vote. Then, I read about the Archdiocese of Kansas City giving over three million dollars to reject a constitutional amendment on abortion in Kansas in 2022. If that is not enough to ponder, the Catholic Church in Michigan gave at least $6M to defeat a similar amendment that same year. In 2023, the Ohio Catholic dioceses gave $1.7M to defeat another constitutional amendment on abortion. All failed.

Why are Catholics losing a connection with their church? I just gave you over 10 million reasons! Poor urban and rural Catholics could have benefited from this money taken from the Sunday collections. If these contributions for political purposes would have been taxed, would the Church still had given the money?

The problem with a growing number of good Catholics is that the Church demands compliance with doctrine with no direct link to Jesus. The most contentious of these doctrines deal with sex. It doesn't matter if it is pre-marital, LGBTQ, or birth control. The Church vigorously opposes all.

Abortion is framed as the killing of a person. The laity views this stance as insulting and an infringement on a very personal decision with possible health implications. The women of the Church (and many men agree) do not want anyone making decisions related to their bodies. The hierarchy doesn't seem to get that. The Church seems to prefer to align with opportunist politicians over its parishioners. (Or, is it the other way around?) Additionally, the Church fails to recognize a significant majority of Catholics are in favor of the right to choose. The message comes across to laypeople that the Church does not respect a woman's ability to reason.

Before I began these essays most of the more controversial doctrines of the Church never appeared on my radar. I suspect most Catholics are like me. I am not a perfect Catholic, not even close. The spiritual experience of being part of the Church is totally satisfying for me.

---

[137] The teachings of the Catholic Church that have been passed down by the successors of the Apostles.

The metamorphosis for me happened at a snail's pace, and as the Church increased its focus on wedge issues and politics, the rate of change accelerated. One of the early signs of the Church straying from its mission occurred almost thirty years ago at my former parish during a Sunday Mass. The pastor passed around a clipboard, a petition of sort, for my signature in opposition to abortion. I sent it along without signing. In the pew in front of me was a local doctor. He seemed to be struggling with the choice to sign or not. Eventually, he began to write. I was appalled by ,and angry with, the attempt to apply pressure at a time reserved for Jesus.

The next stage came via a letter from the bishop imploring me to back some outside-the-scope initiative supported by the Church. Over the years, more communication arrived telling me how I should think. These attempts to influence me were no less an assault on me. I resent (and always will) pressure from the institution chartered to help me be a better human. The time is now for the Church to concentrate on its mission.

Essay 121

8 December 2023

Shalom

(*Peace Be with You*)

In English, Shalom means "peace". Western countries, like the United States, use this translation to define an absence of conflict. Modern day Israel uses it as a hello and goodbye. In Hebrew, the word translated as "well-being", "well", and "in good health". Another Hebrew translation focuses on completeness and tranquility. Father Ott[138], during his homily on a Sunday awhile back, defined Shalom to mean "may everything be as it should be" or "may everything be as God wants it to be".

"May everything be as it should be". Is that the status quo? In my life I tried (mostly without success) to avoid change. Turns out, the change was good for me. Father Ott, in his definition of Shalom, hits the nail squarely on the head. It's about doing the right thing even under enormous encouragement to do the opposite. It's right versus wrong. Good versus evil. When we are true to our moral and ethical compass, things are as they 'should be'.

Since I am writing this essay around Christmas time of 2023, defining Shalom as "peace" seems appropriate. This time of year, we celebrate the birth of Jesus and all the hope it brings to us. There are crises all over the world; Ukraine and Gaza are on the front pages of newspapers everywhere. Ideologies threaten to upend the fragile balance between freedom and totalitarianism. It's almost winter time and city governments around the U.S. are in the process of dismantling the modern day "Hoovervilles" with no good plans for relocating the homeless. While many kids are anticipating bundles of presents under the tree, other children are hoping to have something to eat on Christmas Day. Contrary to what the song tells us, "It's a great day to be alive"[139], it could be a lot better.

Now that I turned you smile into a frown, Christmas always brings hope for a better time. Shalom. *"Peace be with you"*[140]. I will remain optimistic for peace in Ukraine and the Middle East. I will remain optimistic for the homeless to find refuge and peace. I will remain optimistic that kids will find a present under the tree. I will remain optimistic that our better angels prevail and we return to *"one nation, indivisible, with liberty and justice for all"*.

Shalom and Merry Christmas to all.

---

[138] Mark S. Ott. Professor. Saint Mary Seminary & Graduate School of Theology, Wickliffe, Ohio.

[139] A song performed by Travis Tritt and written by Darrell Scott.

[140] **[Jn 20:19]**

Essay 122

15 December 2023

Good Samaritan

A scribe asked Jesus, "And who is my neighbor?" He replied with a parable. *"A man fell victim to robbers as he went down from Jerusalem to Jericho. They stripped and beat him and went off leaving him half-dead. A priest happened to be going down that road, but when he saw him, he passed by on the opposite side. Likewise, a Levite came to the place, and when he saw him, he passed by on the opposite side. But a Samaritan traveler who came upon him was moved with compassion at the sight. He approached the victim, poured oil and wine over his wounds and bandaged them. Then he lifted him up on his own animal, took him to an inn and cared for him. The next day he took out two silver coins and gave them to the innkeeper with the instruction, 'Take care of him. If you spend more than what I have given you, I shall repay you on my way back.' Which of these three, in your opinion, was neighbor to the robbers' victim?"* He answered, "The one who treated him with mercy". Jesus said to him, *"Go and do likewise"*.[141]

In a world of bitter divides, it's uplifting to read a story about a human taking the time to care for another. I think we all can agree there are far too many of us that don't show the same compassion for a neighbor.

Before exploring the refusal of the priest and Levite to help, understanding the friction between the Jews and the Samaritans is important to the story. The bickering was not about a territorial dispute. The disagreement was not trivial, it was over the place God chose to make his presence known on earth. The Samaritans believe God dwells on Mount Gerizim, near present day Nablus in the West Bank.[142] Jews believe God chose his habitat to be near Jerusalem.[143]

Like other perplexing squabbles, the Jewish-Samaritan feud was not about a place, rather it was over the people God deemed to be extraordinary. If the Samaritans were correct, then the Jews could not lay claim to be the "chosen people".

The presence of Jesus should have settled the issue, but since Jews do not believe he is the Messiah; God will always reside on Mount Zion and they are uniquely special. Most of us believe we are all God's amazing people; not just Christians or followers of Islam or Judaism. It's silly to believe one's faith is preferred over another by God.

What about the priest and Levite? The priest in the story was most likely a Levite. When the Jews receive the law of Moses, only males from the tribe of Levi could be a priest. These priests would be intermediaries between the Israelites and God. They were responsible for the tabernacle and temple. Only priests were permitted to enter the Holy Place in the tabernacle on Yom Kippur (Day of Atonement)[144].

---

[141] [Lk 10:29-37]

[142] [Duet 11:29]

[143] [Is 8:18]

Within the Levite community, there was a group commissioned to perform duties such as temple guards, caretakers of the sanctuary, and interpreters (teachers) of the law. The Levite in the story was a member of this group.

Some researchers defend the priest for failing to help the severely injured man by citing a long-standing rule in Jewish culture forbidding contact with a dead body. Since the man appeared lifeless, the priest rightly avoided touching the corpse to remain ritually clean. This was the justification for ignoring the man. This argument runs counter to Jewish law that preserving human life supersedes any religious consideration in Judaism.

The real message from the story is about kindness and compassion. To that end, I would like to share a couple of personal experiences.

A few days ago, Debbie and I left a restaurant in shopping plaza that also housed a grocery store. As we approached our car, a lady parked next to us was loading bags. She was leaning on the cart and appeared in distress. Debbie asked her if she was okay and received no response. We returned the cart to the store for her. As we backed out of the parking space, the lady was behind the wheel in the car. She looked in more misery. As we drove off, Debbie wonder if we should have asked to call someone for her.

What Debbie did for another person was commendable. Did we do enough? No, we should have asked to do more.

Situations like the lady in agony are difficult for me. If she had fallen or appeared seriously injured, I react the right way. But, when a person does not ask for help, most times I do nothing. I view it as an infringement on their personal space. That's not the way I want to be or act. Overcoming quirky personality traits is a challenge for me. I need to be better.

Another example along the lines of becoming involved without an invitation is a car accident. Have you ever come upon a car in a ditch and continued driving? I have, more than once. These personal challenges happen when a good Samaritan had already stopped or was about to. I rationalize my lack of involvement by convincing myself that assistance was already there to help the victim. How did I know that?

Jesus was asked by a scribe what was the most important commandment. After answering the interrogator, Jesus offered some unsolicited advice about the second most important of the commandment. He said, *"You shall love your neighbor as yourself."*[145] That's exactly what the guy did on the road from Jerusalem to Jericho.

---

[144] Day of Atonement, Yom Kippur, is the holiest day of the Jewish year.
[145] **[Mk 12:28-34]**

Essay 123

22 December 2023

The Good Shepherd

Jesus said, *"I am the good shepherd, and I know mine and mine know me . . . I will lay down my life for the sheep."* [146]

We are the "sheep". Jesus leads us from darkness to light. He surrendered earthly life for us. His death freed us from our sins. What more can we ask of him? What more can we do for him?

For the moment, I would like to defer a discussion of spiritual leadership until later in this essay and focus on what makes a good leader. The first characteristic of effective leadership is the ability to influence others. This is accomplished by articulating a clear vision while making the necessary behavioral changes to achieve it.

The second attribute is trust. Transparency is essential to build trust. Clearly communicating organizational goals and challenges help stakeholders understand the way forward. The next step is to demonstrate how stakeholders contribute to the success along with emphasizing accountability from top to bottom.

Managed risk taking by a leader encourages innovation. A culture that inspires others to "think outside the box" embraces creativity. When norms are challenged, great things happen. The fifth characteristic of leadership is integrity. Without honor, a leader has no moral compass. Integrity and impeccable ethics are the most important qualities of a leader.

The sixth pillar of a leader is to act decisively. Strategic decisions often determine success or failure. Preparation is essential, but when the decision is made, a leader moves quickly. Maintaining a resolve to navigate the ups and downs of a decision is vital. If there is a compelling reason to change—do it. The last characteristic of an effective leader is resiliency. Not all decisions end in success. Recovering from failed ventures demonstrate the ability to respond to adversity while sustaining a focus on the goal.

An effective leader is a "good shepherd". Let me pose a question to you, is Jesus the model for the management theorists in identifying the traits of an effective leader?

Let's explore.

To be a "good shepherd", Jesus needed to influence people to do the right thing when options were available. In the Gospel of Mark, Jesus observed people making charitable contributions to a cause. The wealthy gave large sums while the poor gave meager amounts. He gathered his disciples and said, *"Amen, I say to you, this poor widow put in more than all the other contributors to the treasury. For they have all contributed from their surplus wealth, but she, from her poverty . . .* [147] People with "means" rarely consider what is right giving.

Jesus was a risk taker. The discourse [148] with the woman from Samaria illustrates his willingness to challenge the norm. As Jesus journeyed through Samaria enroute to Galilee, he came to the town of

---

[146] **[Jn 10:11,14-15]**

[147] **[Mk 12:41-44]**

Sychar and decided to rest near Jacob's well[149].   A woman of Samaria came to draw water from the well and Jesus asked for a drink. She responded by saying, "How can you, a Jew, ask me, a Samaritan woman, for a drink?" Jesus flipped the question and cryptically responded by implying if she knew him, then she would be asking for a drink.   The woman said to him, "I know the Messiah is coming, the one called the 'Anointed'; when he comes, he will tell us everything." Jesus said to her, *"I am he, the one who is speaking with you"*.

The woman left her water jar and hurriedly returned to town to share her encounter. She exclaimed, "Come see a man who told me everything I have done. Could he possibly be the Messiah?" Many of the Samaritans went and became believers.

Jesus came from Galilee to John at the Jordan to be baptized by him. John tried to prevent him saying, "I need to be baptized by you, and yet you are coming to me?" Jesus said to him in reply, *"Allow it now, for thus it is fitting for us to fulfill all righteousness."*[150]

Jesus followed the Spirit into the desert to be tempted by the devil. After forty days he was hungry. The tempter approached and said, "If you are the Son of God, command that these stones [to] become loaves of bread." Jesus said in reply, *"It is written: One does not live by bread alone, but by every word that comes forth from the mouth of God."* Next, the devil took him to the holy city and said, "If you are the Son of God, throw yourself down." Jesus answered, *"Again it is written, you shall not put the Lord, your God, to the test."* Finally, the devil promised the world to Jesus if he submitted to him. Jesus, fed up with these temptations, ordered the devil to leave saying, *"It is written: The Lord, your God, shall you worship and him alone shall you serve."*[151]

After reading these teachings of Jesus, is he an effective leader?

Jesus gave his life and forgave our sins (all of them) so that we could have a shot at eternal life. I'm not sure we appreciate or truly understand the significance of what he did for us. Maybe it's because Jesus never directly said to all the sinners of the time, "Hey, you guys have been bad dudes. I'm going to give you another chance and free you from all the wicked thing you did."

Do you need more validation that Jesus is looking out for us? Peter asked Jesus a question: "Lord, if my brother sins against me, how often must I forgive him? As many as seven times?" Jesus answered, *"I say to you, not seven times but seventy-seven times."* [152]

The lesson learned in this essay is that all of us have the capacity to be a "good shepherd". We need to think about others before ourselves. We need to practice compassion and understanding for all humans. Finally, we must always do the right thing regardless how difficult it is to do.

---

[148] [Jn 4:4-7,9-10,25-26,28-29,39-42]

[149] Jacob's well provided a source of water in an arid environment. Symbolically, it represented life. The ancestry of Jacob is linked to Abraham. As adult, Jacob became Israel. The future Jewish state was named for him.

[150] [Mt 3:13-15]

[151] [Mt 4:1-11]

[152] [Mt 18:21-22]

Essay 124

30 December 2023

"I Want to See"

After departing Jericho on his final journey to Jerusalem, Jesus was approached by a blind man seeking mercy. Jesus asked the man, *"What do you want me to do for you?"* Bartimaeus replied, "I want to see", and he did.[153]

"I want to see." What an intriguing thought!

What if I was blind? I sometimes think about that. Would my cup be half empty and feel sorry for myself? Could I handle never knowing what my family or friends look like? Would I even have friends? With all the adaptive technologies out there to help blind people, could I learn to use them?

These questions are written by someone that can see. How would a person that never had the privilege of sight answer? For a blind person It could be a colossal undertaking to just cross the street. But, it's not! It is that "bump in the road" we humans resourcefully learn to navigate around, over, under, or through. The blind or visually impaired learn to master the adaptive tools and do all the things sighted people do. I saw a post from a man named Aaron James on the question-and-answer website Quora. Here's what he wrote:

"I am totally blind and have been since I was born. I have a windows 7 laptop, an iPhone 7, and a white cane. All of which are tools I cannot live without. Back in the 90's, or even early 2000's, things were not as accessible as now. And even now we still have a lot to perfect. I take the bus; I watch TV without description. I listen to music; I love to read and write. I am a great singer. Blindness is something I was born with. It is something that takes a lot to adapt to. But it could always be worse."

All of us with a half empty glass, take that and smoke it in your pipe!

Limitations (I prefer not to use disabilities) are just that, "bumps in the road" of life that the human spirit works to overcome. It's not defining of a blind person (bet you heard that before), it a challenge to prove all the naysayers wrong. The glass is always half full for those refusing to accept things as they are, and instead, seek to achieve goals like any other person.

There is another form of blindness that people refuse "to see" the things right in front of them. The other day, a Republican candidate for president next year—Nikki Haley—was asked the cause of the Civil War. The obvious and correct answer was slavery. Haley responded by saying it was about personal freedoms. The irony of her answer is that she is the daughter of immigrant parents from India. She knows racism firsthand. Why answer as she did? Haley was pandering to white grievance[154] Americans. Where's her courage of conviction?

---

[153] **[Mk 10:46-52]**

[154] White grievance is fear-based panic by a person against immigrants and ethnic minorities. The perception of dominance by whites is waning and economic opportunities are declining. The group is easily influenced for political expedience.

In the Middle East, a radical group of Islamic militants slaughtered a group of Israeli concert goers near the border with the Palestine territory of Gaza in October. Israel retaliated with vengeance. The act of terrorism was a few months ago and the military siege of Gaza continues with no end in sight according to the Israeli government.

The Gaza operation has morphed from a hunt for the perpetrators of the act to the complete annihilation of a people. It is an unimaginable humanitarian crisis. I wonder how the Israeli government justifies their action to God.

The world has condemned the continuing carnage, but stopped short of doing anything about it. The United States, my country, continues to provide cover for Israel along with material support for the campaign. Why? It's politics! Some will justify support because of the geo-political importance of Israel to the expansion of Islamic extremism. My answer to that claim—remember Vietnam.

There is a current movement in some states to modify school curriculums through legislation to restrict the teaching of some American history. Books are being banned for perceived objectionable content. Why is a small minority influencing what kids learn? Again, politics!

"To see" comes with an enormous responsibility. For so long, we have looked the other way. Is it because we don't care? Is it because it doesn't impact us? Is it because we have other things to do like soccer games or vacations or golf? The answers to these questions are YES, YES, and YES.

Let me offer a final thought on the present apathy in our country. Here's a scenario to ponder.

It was Saturday morning and a farmer in north central Pennsylvania went to the nearby town to shop as he has done every week forever. Walking down main street he spits on the sidewalk. There's a law in the town against spitting in public. An old geezer walking on the other side of the street objects to the act and reports him. The farmer was found guilty as charged and spent the next two years in jail for it. If that farmer was your favorite uncle, would you regret being indifferent to small intrusions on your liberties?

I mention several times in other essays about doing the right thing. That can't happen unless we have core principles to guide us. I'm sure you heard someone say he or she knows when the line is crossed and steps up to defend what is right. Another of my favorite expression of values is "he is a principled man". In both examples these folks have defined right from wrong; they have a core set of values. By the way, we all do. It's time for us to lead by example.

Robert Kennedy gave a speech at the University of Kansas in 1968 during his presidential run. He paraphrased a quote from George Bernard Shaw[155] at the end of his remarks he said, "Some people see things as they are and say why? I dream things that never were and say, why not?" I'll end with that.

---

[155] George Bernard Shaw was an Irish playwright, critic, debater, and political activist.

Essay 125

15 January 2024

Uvalde

This essay is about the killing of school kids. Sometimes, we need to be reminded of these tragic events and the hole left in the hearts of mothers, fathers, brothers, sisters, grandparents, and friends. (See **_Postscript #1_** for a list of the mass school shootings in the United States over the last 25 years.)

Another new school year, another mass shooting at a school in America.

On 4 January at Perry High School near Des Moines, Iowa, a sixth-grader was killed and seven others wounded in a school shooting. It was the first mass casualty event of 2024 involving kids at school. The shooter was a student at the high school . Three victims remain hospitalized as of January 8th according to KCCI, a local television station.   Police have not issued a motive for the attack. The shooter committed suicide.

UPDATE#1: A victim, the principal, of the Des Moines school shooting died of his wounds. [156] Dan Marburger was his name and a hero.

UPDATE2: As of 19 September 2024, there have been 50 school shootings in the United States this year.[157]

We have been forced to cope with the assault on students at schools in Sandy Hook, Virgina Tech, and in Parkland among many senseless massacres over the last 25 years in America. Uvalde in Texas was one of the more troubling, not only for the loss of life, but for the response by police and emergency services. The state government, even today, wants the focus to be on mental health of the shooter and not the propagation of guns.

Before exploring the narrative on school safety and guns, a recap of the Uvalde massacre is appropriate.

On 24 May 2022, nineteen children and 2 teachers died at Robb Elementary School in Uvalde, Texas. Another seventeen people were injured; most with gunshot wounds.

Uvalde is a municipality in the county of the same name. It has a population around 25,000. It is located less than 100 miles from San Antonio. Robb Elementary educated over 500 students; mostly Hispanic and disadvantaged economically. The school has been torn down as a result of the mass killings. Too bad, leaving the school as it was after the shooting would serve as a reminder of all the failed efforts to protect Uvalde's children.

The shooter was an 18-year-old and a former student at the school. Earlier in the day, he shot and severely wounding his grandmother. The perpetrator was fatally shot by members of the United States Border Patrol Tactical Unit.

---

[156] 14 January 2024.

[157] Matthews, O'Kruk and Choi. _School shootings in the US: Fast facts_, CNN, 20 Sept 2024.

The shooter was described as being bullied at school and without friends according the Texas Department of Public Safety. Prior to the shooting, warning signs appeared on social media.

The weapon of choice was an AR-15 rifle. It has more power than the handguns used by police. This type of rifle can penetrate body armor. Additionally, this weapon causes extensive damage to the human body. Before any police entered the school, it was reported the shooter discharged 100 rounds at students and teachers. Almost all of the victims were already dead at the time of the breaching of the building.

On the 1-year anniversary of the tragedy, The Texas Tribune[158] published a story to update readers on the Uvalde shooting. The local and state governments were not particularly forthcoming and reluctant to share information. Journalistic resources, including the Tribune, pursued investigations to provide some "sunshine" to the massacre. The inquiries found fault with public safety communication, leadership, and medical care. The delays from inaction likely cost some lives.

The outrage of the senseless killings spread across the United States and the world. The federal government reacted within weeks and passed the "Bipartisan Safer Communities Act." Provisions of the act were modest. Texas, instead of enacting companion legislation, chose to focus on improving school safety and mental health care.

As noted earlier, the indignation for the mass school shooting in Uvalde was immediate and intense. Several groups and organizations issued statements of condemnation. On the day of the massacre the Catholic Church issued a statement: "There have been too many school shootings, too much killing of the innocent . . . each of us also needs to search our souls for ways that we can do more to understand this epidemic of evil and violence and implore our elected officials to help us take action."[159] The phrase from the final sentence, "we can do more", is how most of humanity feels. But what is it that we can do? I will explore that topic later in this essay.

After Sandy Hook, President Obama pledged to do something about mass school shootings. In January of 2013, he offered a plan—"Now is the Time"—to curb gun violence. The blueprint included: 1) closing loopholes in background checks; 2) a ban on military-style assault weapons and high-capacity magazines; 3) initiatives to make schools safer; and 4) greater access to mental health services. The plan was solid, but the obstacles against implementation were considerable and powerful. The "Assault Weapons Ban of 2013" failed to receive a filibuster-proof majority in the U.S. Senate. The proposal never became law.

I have no doubt of the sincerity of President Obama. The gun lobby and its partners continue to resist attempts to weaken the ability of anyone to buy anything associated with weapons.

After Sandy Hook, the mood in the country began to move away from the Second Amendment to the rights of people to live without fear of mass casualty events. Guns, especially the access to assault-style weapons with high-capacity magazines, was the reason. The defenders, the National Rifle Association and gun manufacturers, sensed the shift and launched a blitz to change the narrative. With the right to bear arms moot, the focus turned to the mental health of the shooter. The argument by the gun lobby

---

[158] Méndez, Maria. *Uvalde school shooting: What we know one year later*. The Texas Tribune. Austin, Texas. 24 May 2023.

[159] School Shooting in Uvalde, Texas. U.S. Conference of Catholic Bishops (USCCB). 24 May 2022.

was that a responsible gun owner should not be punished for a sick person. If the mentally challenged logic failed to take root with the public, then give a teacher a gun for self-defense and the protection of students. Wayne LaPierre, executive vice president of the NRA, notoriously said after Sandy Hook, "The only thing that stops a bad guy with a gun, is a good guy with a gun". The arrogance of the gun rights folks was total and received with broad indignation. Twenty-six kids and teachers were killed tragically; the obstructionists showed zero empathy for the victims and family.

Here's a sad commentary on gun violence and mass shooting in America. Since Sandy Hook only a single federal legislative initiative became law! That was the 2022 Bipartisan Safer Communities Act. It provided funding for mental health services, school security; and expanded criminal background checks for firearm purchasers under the age of 21. Anything missing? Yes, the ban on assault weapons.

Some mass shootings get a more attention than others. What does Sandy Hook, Virgina Tech, and Uvalde have in common? You know the answer. Now, how about Austin, Texas (1966), San Luis Obispo County, California (1987), and Orlando, Florida (2016)? See ***Postscript #2*** for the answer.

The Catholic Church in America has consistently supported reasonable measures to address the problem of gun violence. It backs an assault weapons ban; background check for buyers; access to high-capacity magazines; and improved mental health care along with earlier intervention. The Church has appeared at congressional hearings in support of these values. But, its only words, actions are needed.

 The United States Conference of Catholic Bishops (USCCB) said "We can do more", but we do almost nothing. When these mass shootings happen, we are saddened, outraged, and calls for action are loud. After about a week's worth of news cycles, the tragedy fades in its sorrow and intensity. We move on the next big game or the latest rendition of the political circus. It's time to stop and do something.

Let me pose a question to you, what if every Sunday pastor hammered the message of gun violence (and the control of it) to the folks in the pews, and kept doing it until something is done? I'm convinced people will hear the message, agree with it, and coalesce around a movement to force these spineless politicians that do the bidding for the influencers in the shadows to act responsibly for the good of all.

I believe mental competency, or the lack of it, is the primary driver for a person to commit the unthinkable act of killing at a school or other places.

Mass causalities outside the framework of a school are generally motivated by hate. El Paso was about immigration to the U.S. Orlando was about sexual orientation. Pittsburgh was about antisemitism. Charleston and Buffalo were about racism. Most of us agree these events were hate crimes. Additionally, we agree the perpetrators were misguided (a kind explanation), but how many more victims need to be killed before we do something about it?

What do we do? We change the narrative. We know why immigrants come to the United States. We know the solutions. We know why religious intolerance exists and it's not just against Jews; not just here in America. We know what to do.

The rhetoric needs toned down. The sources sparking the hate comes from political leaders by words and actions. When governors of Texas and Florida bus migrates to "sanctuary cities" to demonstrate political opportunism is contrary to the teaching of Jesus and condemned by most religious denominations, but not all. Explain that to me!

Sanctuary means a safe place. Another term for a sanctuary city is a "safe city". As it relates to immigration, it is a city that will not detain (jail) or allow Immigration and Custom Enforcement (ICE) agents to seek out people that may be in the U.S. illegally. The anti-immigration movement has made a safe place for people a bad place.

One of the first things Donald Trump did as president was to take away federal funds from sanctuary cities. It was pure retaliation against political foes. The Biden administration ended the prohibition in May of 2021. If politicians can't show compassion for another human, how can we solve gun violence? The answer is to change the dynamics. By that I mean vote for people that put our children before an ideology or allegiance to special interests.

It's time to return to mass shooting at schools. The local school district where I live has a written policy for any form of harassment or bullying. Most, if not all, schools have similar policies. Although, these policies do a good job of defining unacceptable behaviors in schools, it would be incredulous to believe words prevent students from being harassed, intimidated, or bullied. It happens today and will tomorrow.

Our kids are on the frontline of all forms of harassment. A teacher is the best advocate for a student targeted by a bully. I have no reservation in saying teachers act responsibly and take the appropriate action every time an incident surface. I can also say it much easier to address bullying in elementary schools. Students at that level may not understand what is bullying and its social implications, but know when a student is being unkind to another. They are more willing to tell the teacher than older students.

Bullying in middle and high schools is prevalent. It is a challenge for targets and witnesses to do something. Statistically, only 1 in 5 incidents are reported to authorities. If we look back at our times in school, it is easy to understand why these occurrences go unreported by victims. See ***Postscript #3*** for details of bullying.

It is difficult for our kids to navigate teenage and young adult years. Psychologists tell us about the effects of bullying —depression, low academic performance, anxiety, etc. Targets of bullying are more likely to have mental health and behavior problems. How many of bullied kids end up to be school shooters? The answer is we don't know. Why do these perpetrators never find their way into the system? We do hear about their isolation and past bullying; always after the tragedy.

The Shooter

A school shooter needs the *WILL, MEANS,* and *OPPORTUNITY* to be the perpetrator of the act. The ***WILL*** is the inclination to do the act and the fortitude to carry it out. To understand this resolve we need to know how a person gets there and what are the circumstances that made it possible. Profiles of shooters from ***Postscript #1*** include documented mental illness, isolation, victimized by a bully, no friends, former student, make threats to other students, obsession with mass casualty events, rejection, envy of others, suicidal tendency, drug addiction, and sexual abuse.

Learning what drives a shooter to do the unspeakable is always a post-mortem audit. It is couched in sympathy for the perpetrator's life experiences. We feel for anyone conflicted by demons from within or out. Sorry, I have no compassion for someone that takes the lives of kids (or adults) because of mental health issues. That said, I hope those troubled find help before the goblins take control.

Mental health concerns have moved to the forefront of school shootings. That's good. As I said before, the mental wellness of a shooter is the primary cause of the violence. Saying and believing it does not prevent the next perpetrator from killing innocent kids. If it did, we would have the answer along with the solution to help sick individuals.

To have the **MEANS** is to possess the tools to perform the act forged through the *WILL*. If you don't have access to guns or other weapons, how do you kill 26 students and teachers at Sandy Hook? That's a rhetorical question.

When mass casualty events occur the people and communities where it took place are the strongest advocates for gun control. Sandy Hook is the model for living victims to follow.   I believe change cannot happen until we are personally affected by a tragedy. Sometimes I think it takes a tragedy in a politician's backyard to effect change. What an awful thought.

OPPORTUNITY is the circumstance necessary to perform the act. This is the stage of a mass shooting that demonstrates deliberate intent. It is the plan for accomplishing the *WILL*. It not a random act. Most of the shootings occurred within the school buildings, but not all. At Westside Middle School in Jonesboro, the shooters perched in a wooded area outside the school after pulling the fire alarm. Students were gunned down exiting the building. The perpetrator of the carnage at Cleveland Elementary School in Stockton filled a van full of fireworks, ignited them, and killed kids leaving the building.

We are not naïve to believe mass shootings happen only at school. We remember the supermarket in Buffalo a couple of years ago; the synagogue in Pittsburgh (2018); the Walmart massacre in El Paso in 2019; and, of course, other mass killings. The emotions solicited in us are raw and intense when these things happen. Some want vengeance. Others look for excuses. The voices for gun control are shouted down because of the constitutional guarantee to own a gun. We know the remedy, or think we do. The problem, in my view, is apathy. As the massacre age, our willingness to do what is right fades too. That indifference is laid squarely at our feet. Maybe, just maybe, we will have the courage to do the right thing—school security, intervention, mental health resources, gun restrictions. What we cannot do is place more guns in the schools in the hands of teachers. That's not what teachers do best.

Postscripts

Postscript #1 – Twenty-five Years of Mass School Shootings

(Source: K-12 Drive Shooting Database and Statista).

1. Virginia Tech, Blacksburg, VA (2007). Victims: wounded 23; killed 32. There were six additional non-gunshot injuries included in the "wounded" total. There were two separate attacks on the campus by the shooter using two semi-automatic pistols. The first shooting occurred at a dormitory; two people were killed. The main attack was at a classroom building. The shooter chained the main entrance doors and proceeded to kill people in classrooms and in a stairwell. The carnage was the deadliest mass shooting on an educational campus or facility at any level, EVER! Prior to the attack, the shooter was declared mentally ill and ordered to receive treatment by a judge. Because the shooter was not institutionalized, he was allowed to purchase guns legally. The shooting prompted the state of Virginia to close loopholes that had allowed individuals found to be mentally unsound to purchase handguns without a background check. It also led to the passage of the first major federal gun control legislation (National Instant Criminal Background Check Improvement Act of 2007) in the U.S. since 1994. The law strengthening the background checks. Shooter committed suicide.

2. Sandy Hook Elementary School in Newtown, CT (2012). Victims: wounded 2; killed 26. The shooter murdered his mother prior to going to the school. At least 156 shots were fired from multiple weapons in five minutes. The police recovered a document from the shooter listing the top 500 mass killings with weapons used in the attack. The shooter's mother purchased the guns. Prior (2 years) to the shooting, he cut off contact with his father and brother. He was home-schooled since 8th grade. He was examined by several psychiatrists; took medication for a short time, but was not open to therapy. Shooter committed suicide.

3. Robb Elementary School. See the discussion earlier in this essay.

4. Marjory Stoneman Douglas High School in Parkland, FL (2018). Victims: wounded 17; killed 17. The shooter was a former student. The attack was planned. The weapon used was AR15 rifle. After the attack the shooter exited the building with other students being evacuated. He had a history of mental health issues. Shooter did not post on social media about the plan or shooting. He demonstrated an interest in other school shootings. He was arrested and sentenced to life in prison without parole.

5. Columbine High School in Littleton, CO. (1999) Victims: wounded 24; killed 13. The shooters planned to bomb the school similar to the federal building in Oklahoma City (1995). The bombs were placed in the school, but failed to detonate. The attack was in planning for more than a year. Shooters made previous death threats to students. Shooters committed suicide.

6. Santa Fe High School in Santa Fe, TX (2018). Victims: wounded 13; killed 10. Shooter did not shoot students he liked so they could tell the story. Shooter had extensive planning documents. IEDs[160] were found at school and at shooter's home. His online postings suggested he was "born to kill". He experienced extensive bullying. Shooter committed suicide.

7. Red Lake Senior High School in Red Lake, MN (2005). Victims: wounded 5; killed 8. Shooter killed his grandfather, a tribal police officer, and took a shotgun and handgun plus a ballistic vest to the school. The shooter was obsessed with Columbine and other mass shootings. School officials were aware of violent journal entries about mass shootings. Shooter was bullied. His father committed suicide and mother was severely injured in car accident; placed into custody

---

[160] Improvised Explosive Device

of grandparents. Shooter was on an antidepressant medication at the time of the shooting. Shooter committed suicide.

8. Isla Vista, University of California at Santa Barbara, Santa Barbara, CA (2014). Victims: wounded 13; killed 6. The assailant stabbed three men to death in his apartment. Later, he went to a sorority house, failing to get inside, he shot three women outside, two died. He next drove to a nearby deli and killed a male student inside. He then began to drive through Isla Vista shooting and wounding several pedestrians from his car and striking several others with his car. The self-described motive was to punish women for rejecting him and, out of envy, sexually active men.

9. West Nickel Mines School in Nickel Mines, PA (2006). Victims: wounded 5; killed 6. The shooter barricaded himself inside an Amish schoolhouse with only female students. He tied up the girls and shot them one by one.   The shooter was married with 3 children and no prior history of mental health issues or violence. He stated the reason for the carnage was that a girl had wronged him 20 years ago. Shooter committed suicide.

10. Covenant School in Nashville, TN (2023). Victims: wounded 1; killed 6. The shooter was a transgender man and former student at the school. He entered the school by shooting through a glass side door. The shooter was under care for an emotional disorder. The guns were legally purchased between October 2020 and June 2022. The shooter was killed by police.

11. Northern Illinois University, DeKalb, Il (2018). Victims: wounded 21; killed 5. There were four additional non-gunshot injuries included in the "wounded" total. The shooter, 27 years old, was a 2006 NIU graduate. He opened fire on students in a large auditorium-style lecture hall. The shooter was wearing a T-shirt with the word "Terrorist" imposed over an image of an assault rifle. It was reported he took anti-anxiety and sleep aid medication. The assailant stopped taking psychiatric medication (antidepressant) prior to the assault. A story published in a magazine confirmed his history of mental illness and alleged that he had attempted suicide; he was bullied in high school. He demonstrated an interest in previous school shootings. Shooter committed suicide.

12. Westside Middle School in Jonesboro, AR (1998). Victims: wounded 10; killed 5. The shooter, a 13-year-old boy, an accomplice (11-year-old boy) pulled the fire alarm, and fired at students exiting the school. All victims were female. The shooters had 9 weapons and 2000 rounds of ammunition. They fled the scene, but later were apprehended by police. Both were known as bullies. The accomplice was sexually abused at age 6, and at age 12 he abused a 3-year-old girl. They were convicted as juveniles and released at age 21 as required by state law. Soon after release, the shooter was arrested for drug possession, unregistered handgun, and theft.

13. Cleveland Elementary School in Stockton, CA (1989). Victims: wounded 30; killed 5. The morning of the shooting an anonymous threat was called into the school. The shooter parked a van full of fireworks near the building and lit it on fire. As the students exited the building, shooter fired on the unsuspecting victims. It was learned he attended Cleveland Elementary School from kindergarten until 7th grade. The shooter was a "troubled drifter" and unemployed. He had a drug addiction and multiple criminal charges relating to weapons and drugs. The weapon of choice was an AK-47, legally purchased in Oregon.

Postscript #2 – Fifty Years Mass Casualty Events

1966 – Austin, TX
University of Texas tower shooting. From a perch at the top of the University of Texas clock tower, a student and former Marine killed 15 people and wounded 31 others before being killed by police.

1986 – Edmond, OK
Edmond post office shooting: A part-time postal employee killed 14 coworkers and wounded 6 before committing suicide.

1987 - San Luis Obispo County, CA
A perpetrator entered the cockpit of Pacific Southwest Airlines flight and killed the pilot, co-pilot, and three other people before crashing the plane. All forty-three passengers and crew on board died.

2009 – Fort Hood, TX
A U.S. army psychiatrist killed 13 and wounded 33 others.

2012 – Auora, CO
At a movie premiere, a shooter killed 12 and wounded 70 others.

2015 – Charleston, SC
A white supremacist killed 9 black people during a prayer service at the Emanuel African Methodist Episcopal Church and wounded 1 other.

2015 – San Bernardino, CA
A married couple opened fire on the husband's colleagues at a work training event killing 14 and wounding 22.

2016 – Orlando, FL
A gunman killed 49 and wounded 53 others at a gay nightclub.

2017 – Las Vegas, NV
A shooter, from the upper floors of a hotel killing 60 people and injuring 867 (411 wounded) others at a country music festival.

2017 – Sutherland Springs, TX
A shooter killed two people outside before entering the church killing 26 and wounding 22.

2018 – Pittsburgh, PA
The shooter killed 11 and wounded 6 at the Tree of Life synagogue. It was an antisemitic attack.

2019 – El Paso, TX
A shooter killed 23 and wounded 22 others at a Walmart Supercenter. The attack was a hate crime against Hispanic immigration.

2022 – Buffalo, NY
The shooter Killed 10 and wounded 3 others at a supermarket. The gunman targeted African-Americans and was influenced by similar terrorist incidents.

Postscript #3 - Bullying

The definition of bullying is any unwanted aggressive behavior(s) by someone in an attempt to gain power of another. It can be an overt act or perceived by the target. This power grab is repeated multiple times or likely to be recurring. Bullying inflict harm or distress on the targeted person including physical, psychological, social, or educational harm. Common types of bullying include physical (hitting, kicking, and tripping); verbal (name-calling and teasing); rumors and group exclusion; and damage to the property of the victim.[161]

---

[161] Source: Center for Disease Control and Prevention

"Stopbullying.gov" is a federal government website managed by the U.S. Department of Health and Human Services. Its mission is to provide information collected from various government agencies on bullying of all forms, prevention of it, and a response to it. The following are information is from the website.

— Profiling a bullying is not easy. Youthful bullies may be socially well connected or marginalized — a loner. A bully, sometimes bully other. Additionally, they me a target of a bully.

— An onlooker that intercedes on the behalf of someone being bullied can make a difference.

— By talking to children about bullying; encouraging to pursue interests; demonstrating kindness and respect; and seeking support to avoid becoming overwhelmed helps.

Rates of Incidence (ages 12-18)

- 20% students report being bullied. (Source: *National Center for Educational Statistics, 2019*)
- 41% of students reported being bullied at school and believe it would happen again. (Source: *National Center for Educational Statistics, 2019*)
- The reasons for being bullied include appearance; race/ethnicity; gender; disability; religion; sexual orientation; made fun of; called names, insulted, the subject of rumors; pushed, shoved, tripped, or spit on; and the intentional exclusion from activities. (Source: *National Center for Educational Statistics, 2019*)
- Bullying occurs anywhere: hallway or stairwell at school; in classroom, in the cafeteria, bathroom, locker room, outside on school grounds, on school buses; online or by text. (Source: *National Center for Educational Statistics, 2019*)
- 46% of bullied at school notify an adult of the incident. (Source: *National Center for Educational Statistics, 2019*)
- 21% tweens (9-12 years old) have been cyberbullied or cyberbullied others. (Source: *Patchin & Hinduja, 2020*)
- Threatened with physical harm. (Source: *stopbullying.gov*)
- Bullies purposely damage or destroyed the personal property of another. (Source: *stopbullying.gov*)
    - onlooker that intercedes on the behalf of someone being bullied can make a difference.
    - By talking to children about bullying; encouraging to pursue interests; demonstrating kindness and respect; and seeking support to avoid becoming overwhelmed helps.
  (Source: National Bullying Prevention Center and stopbullying.gov provides statistical information on bullying.)

Effects of Bullying (ages 12-18)

- Students who experience bullying are at increased risk for depression, anxiety, sleep difficulties, lower academic achievement, and dropping out of school. (Source: *Centers for Disease Control, 2019*)
- Students who are both targets of and engage in bullying behavior are at greater risk for both mental health and behavior problems than students who only bully or are only bullied. (Source: *Centers for Disease Control, 2019*)
- Bullied students indicate that bullying has a negative effect on how they feel about themselves, relationships with friends and family, school work, and physical health. (Source: *National Center for Educational Statistics, 2019*)

Cyberbullying (ages 12-18)

- Cyberbullying is highest among middle school students, followed by high school students, and then primary school students (Source: *Centers for Disease Control, 2019*)
- Types of cyberbullying are hurtful comments and rumors spreading. (Source: *Patchin et al., 2019*)

Essay 126

2 February 2024

School Performance and Funding

Part 1 of 2

Charter School

Public education in the United States is in need of a redo. That's not a revelation to anyone. My blood wants to boil every time I hear the rally cry for school choice.

Let me make it clear; tax dollars for education are for public schools **ONLY** — no charter or parochial or **PRIVATE** schools! State legislatures, the cowards that they are, genuflect to these special interests more times than I care to know.

Charter schools are alternatives to traditional public schools. According to the Pennsylvania Department of Education, a charter school is responsible for improving student learning and opportunities through "innovative teaching methods". Maybe the Commonwealth can share these revolutionary approaches with me and to public school teachers!

Like public schools, charters must comply with state mandates for health and safety, special education, civil rights, student accountability, among other requirements. Additionally, a charter school must meet "measurable academic standards" as defined by the Commonwealth.[162] The Pennsylvania School Board Association provides a side-by-side comparison of public and charter schools mandates. <u>See Chart 1</u>.

Chart 1

Pennsylvania		
Mandate Comparison - Public v. Charter School		
	Public	**Charter**
Enrollment	Inclusive	Selective
School Board	Elected	Appointed
Management	School board	May contract with for-profit entities (EMO)
Programs	Full compliance	Limited compliance
Audit	Yes	No
Certified Teachers	All	75% or greater
Truancy	Yes	No
Transportation*	Yes	No

*Public district must provide busing to charter schools.

Source: PA School Board Association

https://www.psba.org/wp-content/uploads/2014/09/A_Closer_Look-Uneven_Playing_Field-053014.pdf

According to the PSBA, an organization seeking approval to launch a charter school cannot be affiliated with any religious or political group. Furthermore, local districts are required to pay the tuition for every resident-student enrolled at a charter school.   In Pennsylvania (and other states) public school districts are required by law to submit a five-year financial plan. How can a school board effectively work the plan if revenue is in a state of flux because of a potential transfer of funds to charter schools?

The most egregious part of the law allows charter schools to hire a management company to take over operations. These companies are known as an EMO[163], The EMO is a for-profit company. An EMO is

---

[162] PDE: https://www.education.pa.gov/K-12/Charter%20Schools/Pages/What-is-A-Charter-School.aspx#:~:text=Charter%20schools%20were%20created%20to,increase%20learning%20opportunities%20for%20all

not subject to public transparency and accountability laws. If an EMO does not use all the funds received from local districts for a student's education, the difference is their profit. [164]

The approach to charter schools by Ohio is similar to Pennsylvania.

In Ohio a charter school is called a community school. That's like putting "lipstick on a pig"!

Ohio law refers to charter schools as "public schools". The reason given for this is that a charter school is publicly-funded and tuition-free. The similarities end there. Charter schools are privately-operated and take orders from a board of directors not an elected school board. In 1997, charter schools were called "laboratories for innovation".

I wonder how Ohioans feel about their tax dollars going to for-profit companies.

Ohio requires a community school to have a "sponsor" similar to the EMO in Pennsylvania. The school's board of directors must agree to contract with the sponsor to be certified as an alternative school. These sponsors are responsible for the school's compliance with state mandates while providing oversight and technical support. The Ohio Department of Education (ODE) measures a sponsor annually in three categories — academic performance, compliance with laws, and implementation of best practices.

From the inception of alternative schools in Ohio, lawmakers have allowed sponsors and their clients to operate with little oversight. Anytime controls are lacking bad things happen. A case in point involves ECOT[165] and its sponsor, Educational Service Center of Lake Erie West. ECOT overstated enrollment from 2016, maybe longer. ESCLEW ended sponsorship in January 2018. As of June 2022, the Columbus Dispatch reported ECOT owes the state $106.6M and the Attorney General's office another $10.6M. Furthermore, the FBI is involved and has subpoenaed nearly 20 years of campaign contribution records for the ECOT.[166]

The state's rating system for sponsors gave Educational Service Center of Lake Erie West an overall score of "effective" during the ECOT debacle. In the area of compliance with rules and laws, ESCLEW was graded "exemplary".

The Columbus Dispatch offered an opinion article in 2023 about the present state of charter school in Ohio. If you are interested here is the link:
https://www.dispatch.com/story/opinion/columns/guest/2023/06/14/ohio-charter-schools-should-not-be-trusted-with-taxpayer-money-opinion-fordham-institute-columbus/70305673007/.

---

[163] Education Management Organization.

[164] https://www.pacharterchange.org/understanding-pennsylvania-charter-schools/#:~:text=Charter%20schools%20are%20governed%20by,sit%20on%20multiple%20charter%20boards.

[165] Electronic Classroom of Tomorrow.

[166] Source: Article, Columbus Dispatch, 28June2022.

School performance

How do we know our kids are being educated to reach their maximum potential? The U.S. Department of Education and individual states measure the achievement of students from kindergarten through graduation. With progress data, educators can tailor curriculums and tactics to influence outcomes while preparing students for success.

In 2015, Every Student Succeeds Act (ESSA) became a federal law. It reauthorized the 50-year-old Elementary and Secondary Education Act (ESEA) and replaced the No Child Left Behind (NCLB) Act of 2002. The goal of the law was to prepare all students for college and careers.

ESSA requires states to test students in reading and math every year from third through eighth grade and once in high school. In Ohio, language arts and math knowledge are tested as required by ESSA; beginning in fifth through eighth grades testing is expanded to include science. High school students take end-of-course tests in English, math, science, history, and government.

A second tool available to understand student competency is called the National Assessment of Educational Progress (NAEP). It is a measurement of the progress of students in public and private schools in the United States. It is congressionally mandated and known as The Nation's Report Card. Among the subjects evaluated are arts, civics, economics, geography, mathematics, reading, science, technology and engineering literacy, U.S. history, and writing.

Chart 2 shows the report card for 2022 for Florida, New Mexico, Ohio, and Pennsylvania. For a description of NAEP Achievement Levels go to:
https://nces.ed.gov/nationsreportcard/guides/scores_achv.aspx

Chart 2

2022 The Nation's Report Card[167]

NAEP Basic Level or above

	Nat'l	OH	PA	FL	NM
NAEP Math Scores - 8th Grade	61%	64%	61%	58%	45%
NAEP Reading Scores - 8th Grade	68%	71%	67%	68%	57%

NAEP Proficient Level or above

	Nat'l	OH	PA	FL	NM
NAEP Math Scores - 8th Grade	26%	29%	27%	23%	13%
NAEP Reading Scores - 8th Grade	29%	33%	30%	29%	18%

Source: National Assessment of Educational Progress

U.S. News and World Report rank schools in the U.S. The publication is one of many that conduct studies evaluating the state of education in the country. The evaluations usually carry a bias, but the data does provide insight into how kids in different places perform. Why is New Jersey kids achieving

---

[167] These links to NAEP Report Card (https://www.nationsreportcard.gov/mathematics/sample-questions/?grade=8) and grade level achievement criteria (https://nces.ed.gov/nationsreportcard/mathematics/achieve.aspx#grade8) explains in detail the process.

exceptionally well, but New Mexico kids are doing poorly? It's not money. New Mexico funds education about average compared to other states. See <u>Chart 3</u> for the results of the study for selected states.

Chart 3

2023 Best States - Education	NJ	FL	PA	OH	NM
Pre-K-12	1	14	19	21	50
NAEP Math Scores - 8th Grade	1	32	22	19	50
NAEP Reading Scores - 8th Grade	1	21	26	10	50
H.S. Graduation	4	9	23	28	48
College Readiness	3	15	20	22	50

Source: Pre-K-12, Education, Best States 2023 Ranking, US News and World Report, 2023

New Mexico's demographics are dramatically different from New Jersey. New Mexico is about 35% white while New Jersey is 70%. New Mexico is 50% Hispanics; New Jersey is 22%. New Jersey is 15% Black; New Mexico is 3%. Native Americans in New Mexico makes up about 11% of the population; New Jersey less than 1%. Asians are equally split at 10%. Why all these numbers—to illustrate the complexity of the problem. We have a lot of work ahead to bring equal and quality education to all.

Ohio State Testing (OST) is comprised of seven core subjects: Algebra I and geometry (or integrated math I and II); Biology; American history; American government; and English I&II. To meet the standards, the Department of Education defines proficiency as a score of 700 or higher for all tests and indicates the student has met the state standards for that subject and/or grade level. A score of 700 is considered "average". It might be me, but my hope for all graduating students from Ohio schools is to be way more than just average. <u>Chart 4</u> shows the scores from the 2022-23 school year for public and community (charter) sectors.

Chart 4

2022-23 Ohio State Testing: At or Above Proficiency Standard									
	4th Grade		8th Grade			High School			
Schools	LA	Math	LA	Math	Science	Algebra I	Gov't	Am Hist	Biology
Public	73.5%	69.7%	64.3%	80.0%	92.3%	71.8%	81.3%	85.1%	83.3%
Community	31.2%	32.1%	36.6%	22.4%	37.7%	23.2%	55.4%	52.5%	44.6%

Source: 2022-23 Ohio State Testing: At or Above Proficiency Standard.

Pursuing this topic, I expected it would come down to public v. charter school; which option produced the better outcome for the student. I will offer my thoughts on that subject later, but the cumulative performance by 8th graders in math proficiency (<u>See Chart 2</u>) across the country is disturbing. As a parent, knowing my kid could be one of the three students performing below expectation forces me to look inward and at the system. We all want our kids to have the tools to compete globally. So, who is at fault?

The "low hanging fruit" will always be the teacher. It makes no difference if the books have pages torn out of them or the school has two laptops for a class of 30 or the majority of the kids have lunch subsidies. What about that kid that brings a loaded gun to school? It must be the teacher's fault why Johnny can't learn!

School safety will always be a concern. We know more cops or teachers with guns will not prevent the next school shooting. Unfortunately, that's the solution politicians put forward every time something bad happens. Band-aids are all we have to offer.

An example of these half-measures is the recent decision by David Zubik, bishop of the Diocese of Pittsburgh, to employ armed officers in every Catholic school. According to a January 24, 2024 article in the Pittsburgh Post-Gazette, the announcement came after a series of 911 calls falsely reported active shooters last spring at Oakland and Central Catholic high schools. The diocesan security expert was quick to point out the decision to ramp up security at schools was not in direct response to the "swatting" incidents. Believe that? I have a bridge in Arizona to sell you!

Security is getting better. Buildings are becoming more secure along with regular active shooter drills. All this is good, but it comes at the expense of classroom instruction. State budgets are formulated in a vacuum. Legislatures are forced to fund education with an eye to the next election. The dilmena faced is how to fix the education system when people are calling for cut taxes. We have come to learn how that shakes out.

So, what do we do? It's not more charter schools. It's not razor-wire circling the schools. Teachers can do a better job, but that is not the problem. It's more money and the more efficient use of it. There needs to be an honest dialogue between funders, decisionmakers, taxpayers, and us.

Educating is a shared value. It's not just for families with children in PreK through 12 grade. Too many times we hear voices shouting about not having "a dog in the fight". Hey stupid, you probably have grandchildren that are or will be in the system soon. We all are vested in giving a kid the best tools to succeed. Until we acknowledge that fact, math scores will remain a challenge.

Charter schools. As the scores nationally and in Ohio show, charter school students are not benefiting from what is marketed as a safer and innovating environment. Actually, the scores do a disservice to the kids attending these schools. Most charter schools are located in urban areas full of poverty and crime. Close your eyes and imagine you are the kid darting and weaving through a crowd of bullies and drug agents at the entrance to the school. From there, you are stopped from passing through a metal detector because someone in front of the line had a gun. Eventually, you make it to the classroom and found a window broken in the door. Finally, you make it to a desk with a chair, and ready to learn. Now, be transported back to your safe place; you wonder how a kid could ever learn anything?

As resources are diverted from public schools, we expect good things. When that doesn't happen, fix the public schools.

I don't have a good opinion of charter schools, especially the motive of some operations. I know there must be some good charters out there with the best interests of the kids at heart. But when I think of the operators, the word huckster is top-of-mind.

Here's a question for all, if a student's performance is the same for public or charter schools, why can't public school decisionmakers identify the reasons for transferring to a charter in the first place? The answer is easy, but remedies are a heavy load.

Thanks for reading. Part 2 of schools is the next essay. The focus is on school funding.

Essay 127

9 February 2024

School Performance and Funding

Part 2 of 2

School funding

The Ohio school funding formula is complicated. It begins with a fixed cost for education based on the total number of students expected to be in the public school system. A key component of the funding model is the relative wealth of the district. In a nutshell, wealthier districts are expected to pay a larger portion of the cost to educate while less effluent areas receive additional state funds to compensate for shortcomings. The money in the state education budget comes from federal (10%), state (45%), and local (45%) sources. For the 2023-24 school year, the dollars for each student attending public and charter schools were almost $12,000.

In 2023, there were over 600 public school districts and more than 250 charter schools in Ohio. Charter schools enrolled about 120,000 students. The students attending charters come from public schools not the private sector.

As the non-public school sector expands (anticipated growth is 5% annually) and funding for education remains stagnant, student performance will do the same.

As noted in **Part 1** of this essay, Ohio charter schools must have a sponsor to operate. But, how do sponsors make money? When a charter school decides to enter into an agreement with a sponsor, almost all allotted funds are assigned to the management company. According to a report in the Columbus Dispatch, the sponsor can keep up to 3% of the charter school funds without an explanation for how these fees are earned.

Let's assume the sponsor realizes the maximum 3% per student for services. That's over $40M annually or $350 of lost educational opportunity for every student enrolled at the charters. It's unlikely that sponsors achieve the full 3%, but any amount of taxpayer dollars funneled through non-profit organizations to for-profit partners is wrong and probably illegal.

What about parochial and private schools in Ohio? Don't worry, these schools get a piece of the pie! The argument is framed as the right of a taxpayer to have a say in how their property taxes are used for education. It's called school choice.

School choice is a voucher program known as an EdChoice Scholarship in Ohio. The program provides students an opportunity to attend participating private schools. The scholarship is based on household income.   It must be used to attend private schools that meet state requirements for program participation. Every Catholic school in northeast Ohio meets the guidelines.

The current EdChoice Scholarship provides $6,165 for K through 8th and $8,407 for 9th through 12th grades.[168] The Ohio Department of Education states that payment to a private school cannot be more than the actual tuition. Anyone know of a private high school's tuition that is less than $8,407?

---

[168] Source: EdChoice

How does EdChoice scholarships work? Students from families at or below 450% ($135,000 for a family of four) of the federal poverty level (FPL) receive a full voucher. Families in higher income brackets receive reduced voucher amounts.   For example, a family earning $205,000 (550% of FPL) will receive a K–8 scholarship equal to one-half the full scholarship ($3,083). At 650% of FPL ($240,000 for a family of four) the voucher equals one-fourth of the full amount ($1,541 in grades K–8).[169]

The program does not exclude families in even higher income brackets. A family of four making at least $280,000 can receive a voucher worth $950 for the 2023-24 school year.

The scholarship program requires a private school to accept the voucher as full tuition for students whose families are at or below 200% ($75,000) of the federal poverty level (FPL). Good luck getting accepted!

Here's some interesting statistics from EdChoice. In school year 2022-23, 39,028 students received vouchers. The average voucher was worth $6,036.[170] Each student in Ohio public schools (1.7M) received $135 less for classroom instruction because of vouchers. Seems almost insignificant until we do the math; private schools are robbing $235M from public education.

Chart 5 is a sampling of private parochial schools in the Cleveland Metro area. Four of the five schools are noted for their athletic programs. To the surprise of few, athletic grants are not part of public information. I suspect, an athlete receives a generous package to attend.

Chart 5

Select Private Schools in Northeast Ohio						
School	Affiliation	Type	Grades	Tuition & Fees	Other Help	EdChoice
Gilmour Academy	Catholic	Co-Ed	9-12	40,350	$2,500 to $30,000	$8,407
St. Edward High School	Catholic	Male	9-12	19,600	$1,000 to $6,000	$8,407
Saint Ignatius High School	Catholic	Male	9-12	19,500	$3,000 to $6,000	$8,407
Magnificat High School	Catholic	Female	9-12	18,500	0 to $5,000	$8,407
Walsh Jesuit High School	Catholic	Co-Ed	9-12	14,925	0 to $9,000	$8,407

A funding crisis at home

Medina City Schools is currently operating at a deficit of about $1,900 per student. The district receives $10,400 (Chart 6) from all funding sources this year. Because of the shortfall, the district has been placed in "precaution status" by the Ohio Department of Education. That means district's taxpayers must pony up or cut educational opportunities to balance the budget. Neither option is desirable. Medina will go to the voters this March to ask for supplemental funds.

Chart 6

	2022-23 School Year - Medina City Schools						
	Actual PPE	State EPP	Delta	% Diff	State EPP 41.6%	Local EPP 48.7%	Federal EPP 9.7%
Medina	12,284	10,396	1,888	15.4%	5,115	5,979	1,190

PPE = Per Pupil Expenditure
EPP = Expenditure Per Pupil
Source: Ohio School Report Cards

---

[169] Source: Thomas A. Fordham Institute

[170] Source: EdChoice

Medina's deficit is approximately $13M. The proposed tax increase would generate enough money to balance the budget. To the homeowner in Medina City School District, it is a tax increase of about $250 a year for $100,000 of assessed property value of for the life of the levy.

What a way to guarantee a child receives a quality education! There's got to be a better way to fund education in Ohio.

In 2022, the Economic Policy Institute published a position paper on public education funding. Give it a read.
https://www.epi.org/publication/public-education-funding-in-the-us-needs-an-overhaul/

Remember when a parent's wish was for their children was to achieve more than they did? I do. I'm not sure that mindset exists today. Paying it forward so that our grandchildren receive the tools to succeed has morphed into a revolt against "tax and spend"[171] policies.

As noted earlier, the Medina dilemma is a result of the funding model.   It is also a product of innovation. By that I mean school decisionmakers (and parents) want to ride the wave of cutting-edge technology, the best facilities, and a curriculum for the gifted—few as they may be. When a fiscal crisis happens, skeptical taxpayers, leery of all these gadgets, are reluctant to chip in and help.

The voices behind lower taxes and abdication of civic responsibility for the greater good, wait, it is me and you—Baby Boomers! Our parents that endured a Great Depression and fought a world war against tyrants would be appalled how we turned out.

Baby Boomers ushered in a social revolution that forever changed society. Somewhere along the way, boomers developed "what's in it for me" attitude. From challenging the norms, we turned inward and became known as the "Me" Generation. What happen to the idealism of our youth? It vanished as we became more materialistic.

Millennials are our children. This generation inherited our self-absorption while exacerbating their own selfishness. As a result, they are called the "Me Me Me" Generation. There is some sunshine though. Millennials believe in social and economic responsibility to improve life outcomes. As the most educated generation in history, knowledge is a valued attribute. Will millennials wake up before it's too late for the kids currently moving through the system? I hope so.

There is a social media platform called "Nextdoor" that is used to connect neighbors in and around Medina. Like Facebook or X, it provides a place to offer opinions and vent among other things. The levy has been a hot topic on it.

The bulk of the comments are negative and misinformation is rampant. For example, most say if the levy passes property taxes will increase dramatically placing an undue burden on seniors. The truth is that the property tax is calculated on the assessed value of the home, not the market value. The taxable value for the property is about 1/3 of the appraised value.

The opponents of school funding are close-minded about education and other things. School boards have little chance of convincing these folks of the value of providing a quality education to meet the demand of globalization.

In an earlier essay, I used analogy to illustrate a point. It is applicable for this discussion too. When asking for a steak sauce at a restaurant, the customer usually say A-1. When the school board says levy for quality education, others hear taxes.

---

[171] A term used in politics meaning government policy to increase or collect taxes for the purpose of increasing public spending.

School decisionmakers are not without blame. These folks believe the need is real and the necessary reductions are well thought out if a levy does not pass. They may be, but the perception of the service cuts is what matters. On the district's website, there is a list of what could happen with a failed levy. The listed is headed by "Reductions potentially could include" blah, blah, blah. Why use the word "POTENTIALLY", the board and administration said it needs $14M to keep the status quo, but if the levy fails a detailed plan is discretionary? That's perception!

I remember another levy Medina schools pushed about 10 years ago. The levy was in trouble until the board threatened the closure of a neighborhood school if it didn't pass. That school was my neighborhood school. The 500 or so student-families in the Heritage area voted in favor of the funding to preserve our neighborhood school. It passed and the school remained open.

Intimidation works in the short term, but erodes confidence in the ability of decisionmakers to govern. That's part of the problem facing the current levy. This time there are "hot button" issues tailored for almost every family – eliminating gifted programs and advance placement classes; cutting back on school resource officers (cops with guns); elimination of some busing, and pay-to-play increases.

Busing is the district's "red herring". If levy fails and busing moves to the two-mile state minimum, some kids will be forced to cross two busy state routes and a U.S. highway to get to school. I believe the board understands the emptiness of the threat.

An update about Heritage; the school will close at the end of this year regardless of the outcome of the levy. The reason cited is the decrease in enrollment. The levy that protected Heritage funded three new schools. The board was forced to redistrict to fill these new schools. Coincidence or planned? By the way, Heritage is the top-rated elementary school in the district.

When the time comes to critique the current school funding effort in Medina, the message to the school board and the administration is that it is imperative to be forthcoming with the voters to build trust. Without it, the cycle of failed levies and threatened cuts to education will continue.

> **Update**: The levy to provide funding for the Medina City School District was defeated by a vote of 52.6% to 47.4%. In November of 2024, the Board of Education will ask voters to approve a similar levy. This will be the 3rd consecutive election cycle for requesting additional operating funds.

I have alluded to the funding model as the problem in Ohio. It is and the state will continue to fall short of meeting the obligation to a quality education for all. Why? Part of the problem is the legislature will always pander to the voices for low taxes. It doesn't matter the purpose for the tax, just that it must be lower or eliminated.

Ohio wants funding to be a shared responsibility between the state and local jurisdictions receiving the benefit. That means a school district like Medina needs to come up with about 50% of the cost.

The role of the federal government is minimized by states for fear of ceding control. As a result, federal funding to schools is limited to congressionally mandated programs like Title I, IDEA (Disabilities), etc.

School districts are required to follow the lead of the Ohio DOE regarding testing, graduation requirements, and other mandates. Local districts have some control over curriculum, but must follow state guidelines. Now, tell me if Ohio dictates how schools operate, why is the cost to educate an equally shared responsibility with local communities? Why doesn't the federal government have more influence in education at the neighborhood school? The Feds have the tools and a vested interest to educate its citizens; so why not pay the total education bill?

The reason is the 10th Amendment to the U.S. Constitution — "The powers not delegated to the United States by the Constitution, nor prohibited by it to the States, are reserved to the States respectively, or to the people." This is the basis for making education a function of the states.

". . . or to the people." The Amendment allows it. If the states want to dictate, a significantly greater financial commitment is necessary. That would alleviate the property tax pressure. If the legislature balks at that, then make education the province of the federal government. It's time to change.

 Intelligence.com rated states according to educational performance. In the category of "Academic Performance", the top five were Massachusetts, New Jersey, Connecticut, Wisconsin, and Virginia. At the other end were Oklahoma, Louisiana, Alaska, Mississippi, and New Mexico. Why can't the kids in Mississippi receive the same opportunity as kids in Massachusetts?

A guarantee of a quality education is not equal opportunity. It is the right of every kid from the high desert of Nevada to the swamps of the Low Country in South Carolina to have the same chance to succeed.

To paraphrase the words of Martin Luter King: ""I have a dream that . . . one day [our kids] . . . will not be judged by [where they live] but by the content of their [knowledge]."[172]

---

[172] King, Martin Luther Jr. Speech, "I Have a Dream", Lincoln Memorial, Washington, D.C., 28 Aug 1963.

Essay 128

2 March 2024

"Blessed are the peacemakers, for they will be called children of God."

Peacemaking is conflict resolution. The person that makes peace is called a peacemaker.   A peacemaker is benevolent, committed, steady, calm, and unyielding in pursuit of the truth.

On every January 1st, the Holy Father provides a special message on the World Day of Peace to encourage people to reflect on the importance of working for peace. Pope Francis celebrated the 55th rendition in 2022 with the theme of building a durable peace. He began his message by calling for a shared commitment to achieve a lasting peace.[173] The Pope laid out a blueprint for peace that reads more like a term paper in a management theory class. It went like this, 1) encourage a dialogue between adversaries: 2) after the parties have exchanged pleasantries, the group identifies shared goals; and 3) keep the process moving forward to build trust among aggressors.

The following is how earthlings may accept the charge from Pope Francis.

> *The good people of earth were enthusiastic and ready to go. A global meeting was schedule for early next year. Everyone wants Francis to be the teacher. He declines the offer preferring another to accept the mantle. He's willing to act as a facilitator, but only until someone steps up to lead the group.*

> *Johnny, known by many for his opinions on about everything, is selected as the leader to develop the plan for peace.*

> *Johnny pursues his calling with vigor. There will be charts strategically placed around the room and handouts for all. The proposal is elementary.   At the get-together, Johnny unveils the first chart to divulge the steps necessary to bring adversaries together as friends in pursuit of peace. The group is excited to a fever pitch by the fervor of Johnny.*

> *The capstone is ready for the big reveal. The cork on the champagne bottle is about to pop! Ready for it? Johnny writes on the chalkboard, "to resolve a disagreement requires* ***"SUPERPOWERS TO USES THEIR INFLUENCE TO END THE DISPUTE".*** *It's Christmas in July — peace on earth and good will to all. Hooray!*

The pundits give Johnny an A+ for the plan I give the plan a big fat "F" for fatuous.

It takes time to achieve an acceptable outcome. Expediency only happens if adversaries are no longer combative. That usually occurs when the cost of continuing the conflict exceeds the benefit gained from it.

---

[173] *Dialogue Between Generations, Education and Work: Tools for Building Lasting Peace,* Message of His Holiness Pope Francis for the Celebration of the 55th World Day of Peace, 1 January 2022.

The pope as an influencer for peace over the last 100 years is mixed. It could be characterized as mostly inconsequential. In the 1930s, Pope Pious XII called on Josef Stalin to stop oppressing Catholics. Stalin responded with "How many divisions has he got?" That, in a nutshell, speaks to a Roman Catholic pontiff's dilmena. The Church has little influence with countries that do not respect Christianity.

During World War II, Pope Pius XII was publicly silent for fear of offending Hitler and Mussolini. The strategy worked; although Italy was 100% occupied at different times by both fascist regimes, the Vatican remained whole, but isolated until the Allies conquered the bad guys a few days before the Normandy invasion.

The reticence and failure of moral leadership during the systematic elimination of European Jews will remain a dark chapter in Roman Catholic history. The Church and European Catholics would prefer us to remember their contributions to aid the persecuted; hiding Jews and their families from the Nazis. Many in Europe did the same and more.

The role of papacy in conflict resolution did succeed in the fight against Communism in Eastern Europe. John Paul II, the first Polish pope, by demonstrating support for anti-authoritarian national social movement known as Solidarity, helped restore democracy to Poland and greased the skids for the end of Soviet Union domination in Europe. His leadership was pivotal.

What does the Pope need to do? First, recognize the present-day adversaries of peace are Russians, Arabs, and Jews. These combatants marginalize Christianity and have no respect for the Vatican. Okay, then what—take a stand! Francis is an influential leader with almost 1.3B followers. If the Church does the right thing and speaks out against a wrong; and speaks out again and again, the world will take notice. As Israel is finding out in Gaza, the Jews are being transformed from the aggrieved to the terrorist. Some of that is because of Francis.

The world needs Francis to lead the crusade for peace. Yes, it is a crusade! It will take an individual with unimpeachable character. That person is Francis.

Earlier, I listed characteristics of a peacemaker. What is a peacemaker? Before defining a peacemaker, let's talk about what it is not. A peacemaker does not sit on the sidelines. A peacemaker does not occupy a director's chair on a movie set. A peacemaker does not use a megaphone. A peacemaker does not show up on Sunday television to brag about accomplishments to date. A peacemaker does not wear designer's clothes; and on, and on, and on.

To be a peacemaker is to respect human life. Peacemakers speak out against injustice. Peacemakers tell the truth. Peacemakers challenge authority to do what is right. Peacemakers expose false narratives. Peacemakers listen. Peacemakers are fearless; and on, and on, and on.

Do you want to be a peacemaker in sheep's clothing or jeans with a hammer loop and a ruler pocket?

Why do we always associate peacemaking with armed conflicts. Peacemakers are needed in other places too.

Global warming is real. It is also a very polarizing. Some believe the demand for goods and profits outweighs the burden placed on the economy from implementing "green" initiatives. Environmentalists suggest time is running out to reverse the consequences from a lack of responsible stewardship. Although there has been some positive movement, the destruction of the planet is moving at a faster pace than conservation measures can undo the harm.

Climate change has been framed successfully in political terms. Anytime momentum builds for taking action to conserve or support innovation, powerful forces with a financial stake in the outcome spend influence dollars to defeat it. Until ocean levels increase and coastal areas become uninhabitable or fertile farm lands become semi-arid, only then will politicians rush to reject their apathy to climate change. Will it be too late?

Essay 129

8 March 2024

Baptize Me

Jesus said, *"Let the children come to me; do not prevent them, for the kingdom of God belongs to such as these."*[174] He said these words near the end of his ministry on the road to Jerusalem. Parents from all over the region traveled with their children to receive a blessing from him. With a touch of his hand, the children received the Holy Spirit.

For me, baptism is the most sacred of the seven sacraments of the Catholic Church.   All, or should I say most, Catholics know the Eucharist is the most important. Makes no difference to me, I will always believe a child needs the best of possible starts to navigate what is ahead for them.

As Christians, we believe to be baptized with water symbolizes a new beginning. The denominations that believe in infant baptism does it that way to rid a newborn of the sins of Adam and Eve. Other sects reject baptizing infants because of their lack of the necessary understanding to profess a belief in Jesus. That's okay.

There seems to be a movement, a trend with some parents, to not baptize their children under any circumstances. I'm troubled with their refusal to do it. Their reasons, I prefer to call it excuses, range from nonbeliever to allowing the child to make the decision as an adult. When I discuss child baptism with deniers (it's not a discussion it is an argument) it usually comes down to a simple question for me; what if your wrong and something happens to your kid? The response received is a bunch of bullpucky! The conversation ends with, "I'm the parent and I can do what I want!" Are you wondering how I know? It happened in my family.

 I don't believe for a New York minute that God would reject a child if not baptized. In the Gospel of Mathew, Jesus said, *". . . Whoever believes and is baptized will be saved; whoever does not believe will be condemned."* Some like to point to these words as to what happens if a person does not receive the sacrament and dies. I don't see it that way. Jesus emphasized the word "believes" as a condition to avoid condemnation. We can be a believer, but not be baptized and still be judged worthy.

How about the parents that baptize because it is expected of them to do it? These parents have a checklist: 1) baptize baby at six weeks; 2) make sure godparents are Catholic, confirmed, and go to church; 3) buy a baptismal gown; 4) invite relatives and friends to the christening; and 5) have a party. Do these parents really understand what's at stake for the baby? I doubt it.

There is a way to baptize against a parent's wish if you have the guts. The Catholic Church, in its Code of Canon Law[175], specifically addresses baptism outside the normal channels. Anyone with the right intention can perform a baptism by pouring water over the candidate's head while saying: *"I baptize you in the name of the Father, and of the Son, and of the Holy Spirit."*[176] I know it works, I did it!

Earlier, I asked the parents of an unbaptized child a question, "what if your wrong". I don't know the answer. As Jesus said, *"Let the children come to me; do not prevent them . . ."* . That's good advice.

---

[174] **[Mk 10:14-15]**

[175] Legal Information Institute, Cornell Law School, Cornell University: Canon law is a body of laws developed for Roman Catholicism to govern church ceremonies, role of clergy, and religious education.

[176] Canon 861.2.

Essay 130

31 March 2024

The Artful Dodger

*****BREAKING NEWS*****

The Catholic Church is a lobbyist; the President of the United States Council of Catholic Bishops told a conservative talk radio host earlier today. Additionally, the bishop revealed their plan for the upcoming election. Every parish priest will use their Homily on November 3rd to encourage parishioners to vote for candidates that will support our position.

(Note: the above is fiction)

I'm fed up with all the mischaracterization and outright lies of political ads on the tube. I turn on Sportsnet Pittsburgh to watch a Pirate game and, between innings, there is ad after ad attacking a candidate with misinformation or fact-checking another's misleading ad. Only occasionally is there a positive message. I can't imagine what it would be to live in a media market that is really nasty.

In 2016, I quit Facebook. Later, I did the same with Twitter after Musk bought it. I posted very seldom, but liked to read what other have to say. I consider myself fortunate to have used social media to reconnect with an old friend before she passed away. But politics ruined all that. What was especially disheartening was so many of the folks I know from West Newton were utterly foul.

Although my disdain for people hating people because they disagree, as I have said in an earlier essay, I loathe it when it comes from the pulpit. If churches were required to pay taxes on their assets and revenues, would they still do it? But they are not—that is, taxed! Religious entities mostly ignore (thumb their noses at) the tax code. Why? It all about enforcement by the tax authorities. Churches have in their pockets spineless politicians that care more about elections than doing the right thing. My message to all churches, stay in your lane!

Enough of my ranting. This essay is about tax-emptions and enforcement.

The IRS defines tax avoidance as "an action taken to lessen tax liability and maximize after-tax income" and tax evasion as "the failure to pay or a deliberate underpayment of taxes."[177] The tax collector is quick to point out avoidance is legal; evasion is not. At the end of the essay, I have a question for you to answer. I hope you get there.

Organizations that provide help to anyone in need and without a profit motive deserves to be exempt from paying taxes. The IRS agrees. For a religious group or a charitable organization intent on influencing election outcomes should have their tax-exempt status revoked by the IRS. The U.S. Tax Code is clear when it comes to involvement in the political process. The key provisions of the tax code as it applies to any tax-exempt organization are1) direct involvement in politics and 2) lobbying elected government officials.

---

[177] https://apps.irs.gov/app/understandingTaxes/whys/thm01/les03/media/ws_ans_thm01_les03.pdf

Churches and their afflicted groups straddle the line of compliance. I'm sure it's an ongoing effort by the leaders to develop work-arounds to avoid losing all the cushy perks they receive from not paying taxes.

How did these rules come about? The Johnson (Lyndon B.) Amendment to the U.S. Tax Code in 1954 prohibits nonprofits from involvement in political campaigns. The statute provided the IRS with the tools to revoke the tax-exempt status from any organization found to violate the requirements.

The Pew Research Center published a study[178] of the lobbying effort of religiously affiliated groups at the federal level. In 1970 there were forty groups; 2012 there were 216. One-in-five religious advocacy organizations work for the interest of the Roman Catholic Church.

Organizations representing religious institutions tend to be funded by those institutions. Examples include Catholic Relief Services and the Association of Catholic Colleges and Universities. Others represent the official interests and positions of a particular denomination, such as the United Church of Christ, the Southern Baptist Convention, United States Conference of Catholic Bishops, and the United Methodist Church's General Board of Church & Society. Funding for these groups come from the religious bodies they represent.

Religion-related think tanks make up about 10% of religious advocacy groups. These groups conduct research and provide policy recommendations on issues relevant to, or supported by religious tradition. For example, the Culture of Life Foundation conducts research on bioethics, family and marriage, and other social issues and aligned with the Catholic Church. Think tanks are funded by donations from individuals and foundations that support their policy positions. The Jewish Institute for National Security Affairs is a think tanks.

On the domestic front, the most commonly addressed issues for think tanks are the relationship between church and state, civil rights, religious liberties, bioethics, life issues (abortion, capital punishment and end-of-life), and family (marriage definition and domestic violence).

According to a collaborative investigation by the Texas Tribune and ProPublica for a story[179] about the IRS enforcement of the law, the IRS track record for enforcing the Johnson Amendment is not good. In over a three-quarters of a century since the statute became law only a small number of religious nonprofits lost their tax-exempt status; no churches were included in revocation.

In 1992, a few days before the presidential election, Branch Ministries in New York ran two full-page ads in USA Today and The Washington Times urging voters to reject Bill Clinton's challenge to George H.W. Bush. As reported by the Texas Tribune and ProPublica, the ads proclaimed: "Christian Beware. Do not put the economy ahead of the Ten Commandments." The ad asserted that Clinton violated scripture by supporting abortion on demand, homosexuality, and the distribution of condoms to teenagers in public schools. Clinton, the ad said, was "openly promoting policies that are in rebellion to God's laws."

The IRS revoked Branch Ministries' tax-exempt status. They appealed the ruling, but the court sided with the IRS. This case is the only publicly known example of the revocation of the tax-exempt status of a church for political activity by the IRS.

The Texas Tribune and ProPublica detailed violations of federal law by 20 churches in 2022.[180] These pastors shrewdly attempted to shirt the prohibition of supporting their preferred candidate by saying, "I

---

[178] Allen D. Hertzke. *"Lobbying for the Faithful: Religious Advocacy Groups in Washington, D.C."*, Pew Forum on Religion & Public Life, Pew Research Center, May 2012.

[179] Jeremy Schwartz and Jessica Priest. *"Churches are breaking the law and endorsing in elections, experts say. The IRS looks the other way"*, The Texas Tribune and ProPublica, 30 Oct 2022.

am not endorsing a candidate, but . . . " According to the published report, their actions were a clear violation of the Johnson Amendment. The following is a sampling of these violations.

Church	Pastor's Comments	Expert
Church #1 Fort Worth, Texas	The pastors expressed support for political candidates at least three times during sermons. In one instance, the pastor said this of a candidate for the state House: "Now, obviously, churches don't endorse candidates, but my name is L@#$%& and I'm a person before I'm a pastor. And as an individual, I endorse [Candidate A]." With Candidate A present, the pastor stated: "We declare [Church #1] is behind you. We declare [Church #1] is praying for you. We declare [Church #1] is supporting you."	"If it's part of the religious services, his disclaimer doesn't work . . . is absolutely an endorsement. If they're doing it in their capacity as pastors, this violates the Johnson Amendment." **IRS: With the candidate in attendance, Section 501(c)(3) does not permit support for, or opposition to, any candidate (including introductions).**
Church #2 Anchorage, Alaska	A pastor introduced a candidate for U.S. Senate to his congregation. After the candidate spoke, the pastor said: "OK, so I want you to know that we're not just gonna be doing an endorsement for Kelly today, even though I am endorsing [candidate] for U.S. Senate. And you can vote for whoever you want. I'm just letting you know who I'm voting for. It's gonna be her."	"That the pastor says he personally endorses the candidate at an official function of the church makes the statement campaign intervention." **IRS: To avoid a conflict with 501(c)(3), all political candidates seeking the same office must receive an opportunity to speak.**
Church #3 Southlake, Texas	The pastor is part of a coordinated effort by a group of Dallas-area pastors to promote specific candidates running for public office. The pastor displayed the names of candidates running for school board and City Council on a screen. He said: "And so we're not," he said: "We're not doing [endorsing a candidate]. But we just thought because they're a member of the family of God, that you might want to know if someone in the family and this family of churches is running."	"This is a new technique, to join a group of like-minded churches and then identify to the congregation anyone who is a member of any of those churches who is a candidate for elected public office . . . even with the disclaimers is still a violation of the Johnson Amendment. . ." **IRS: See note for Church #1.**

How does your church fair with compliance with the IRS rules for tax-exempt status? The easy answer is that it is likely a major violator of the law without facing consequences for its actions. The reason for it, the IRS is handcuffed by politics. Major denominations have enormous power within the halls of Congress. That should not be an excuse for not enforcing the law; however, governing priorities of officeholders prevent enforcement. As the next General Election approaches, I worry about the erosion of democracy if Trump is elected along with like-minded people. Allowing tax-exempt organizations to circumvent the law greases the skids for a loss of our freedoms.

---

[180] Jessica Priest and Jeremy Schwartz. These 20 churches supported political candidates. Experts say they violated federal law, The Texas Tribune and ProPublica, and Chris Morran, ProPublica, 7 Nov 2022.

Is your church a lobbyist?

What about my church? Let take a look by beginning with the clergy sexual abuse scandal.

In 2019, CBS News reported that the Catholic Church has spent $10.6M to fight legislation designed to help victims of sexual abuse by clergy. An example, is the three million dollars spent for lobbying to derail the Child Victims Act in New York state. The lobbying effort failed, and the legislation ultimately became law increasing the time to seek justice. Another $5M lobbying effort, this time in Pennsylvania, to increase the statute of limitations to seek criminal or civil charges against their abusers.[181] The Pennsylvania legislation is stalled in the state Senate. There is no current reporting on additional lobbying dollars spent by the Church.

The Associated Press published a report of the lobbying of religious groups to amend the Paycheck Protection Program part of the CARES Act.[182]   The Catholic Church was part of the effort to persuaded the Trump administration to adjust the eligibility requirement of employees to qualify. Without a redefinition, many Catholic dioceses would have been ineligible to participate. The Catholic News Service reported that the USCCB along with several major Catholic nonprofit agencies worked to change the eligibility. According to Micah Schwartzman, a University of Virginia law professor specializing in constitutional issues and religion, the change was worth billions to the Church.

Federal records show the Los Angeles archdiocese paid $20,000 to lobby the U.S. Senate and House on "eligibility for non-profits" under the CARES Act. Additionally, Catholic Charities USA paid another $30K to lobby on the act and other issues.

Let me say it again; "How many meals, doctor visits, medication refills, rent and utilities subsidies, or crisis interventions would $10.6M pay for in New York?"

Yes, my church is a lobbyist.

The Catholic Church in America, and its dioceses, are big business with all the rewards and risks that come with it. It's wrong to run the church of Saint Peter that way. There is no other way to say it, the Church and its lieutenants need to return to the mission given to the first leader by Jesus.

Remember, I alerted you to a question to come at the end? Before asking it, I looked in Therarsus.com for a little help with a synonym for "evasion". One of the strongest matches is "avoidance". Now, does our religious community avoid or evade taxes—agree or disagree?

Finally, The Free Dictionary by Farlex defines "artful dodger[183]" as a rascal who avoids getting in trouble for their mischief or bad behavior through crafty or resourceful means. Is our religious community an "artful dodger"?

---

[181] Christina Capatides. *"Catholic Church spent $10.6 million to lobby against legislation that would benefit victims of child sex abuse"*, CBS News, 6 June 2019.

[182] Reese Dunklin and Michael Rezendes. *"After lobbying, Catholic Church won $1.4B in virus aid"*, Associated Press, 10 July 2020.

[183] *Farlex Dictionary of Idioms*. S.v. "artful dodger." Retrieved August 17 2024.
https://idioms.thefreedictionary.com/artful+dodger

Essay 131

8 April 2024

Totality

Three minutes and twenty-seven seconds changed me!

Monday, 8 April 2024
1358:42hrs: Eclipse began in Medina
1513:28hrs: Totality began
1515:11hrs: Maximum Totality
1516:55hrs: Totality ends
1628:43hrs: Eclipse ends in Medina

With all the hype during the last month about the solar eclipse being a once in a lifetime event made me a little indifferent about staking out the best place to watch the moon block the sun. In my defense, the airways were inundated with news about it. KDKA evening news reported 97% of the hotels in Erie, Pennsylvania were booked on that day in April. Crazies, dressed like Robin Williams from "My Favorite Orkan", were interviewed by a not so polished reporter in "Podunk, USA" on major network outlets. How about all those weather personalities pretending to be meteorologists giddily telling us the forecast for 1:58pm in Medina on the 99th day of the year of our Lord 2024. Schools closed; not early dismissals, but actually padlocked for the day. Workers called off that day too. I wonder if hospitals postponed surgeries. Only thing missing was another Y2K conspiracy.

There were watch parties all over the place. Medina City sent out a communique to residents and businesses to stock up on food and fill gas tanks for fear of shortages because of all the out-of-towners coming to view Totality. The city also cautioned about traffic congestion in and around town.

Americans, 31 million in all, were in the path of the total eclipse of the sun. How many of these people witness the event — half probably; by July that number will grow to 30, 999, 971. The 29 that still won't admit not viewing the event are Mike Tomlin, his apologists, and Steeler brass!

By the way, I was one of witnesses to cosmic history. Maybe "indifferent" was not the best choice to describe my apathy. How about "stupid". I was privileged (and mean that sincerely) to be an eyewitness to the eclipse.

Bill Mazeroski gave me the best birthday present ever. I saw the Cathedral of Learning in all its splendor at night. I witness Tony Dorsett run on the AstroTurf of Pitt Stadium. I was privileged to live in Western Pennsylvania during the Steel Curtain. I walked across the Clemente Bridge and watched games at the best ballpark in the world. I played Oakmont. I travelled California Highway 1 from San Luis Obispo to the Monterey Peninsula to be awed by the Big Sur; crossed the Bixby Bridge and visited Pebble Beach. I drove across the Golden Gate Bridge in the fog. I even saw a black guy become president. All these experiences never impacted me like the three minutes and twenty-seven seconds on April 8th.

As Totality arrived, I expected to see a dark circle outlined with a gold ring. After all that's the image being peddled by the media and serious science folks. What I experienced was the majesty of the brightest of white light originating from the place in the sky where the sun now was blocked by the moon. WOW!!!!!!!!!!!!!!!!

I began to look for a word or words to describe what just occurred. A "left brainer" like me should be searching for a logical explanation. At that moment, any application of logic was not part of my thought process. It was a spiritual happening! Nothing more needed to said of the alignment of the sun, moon, and earth on April 8th in 2024.

Science will tell us the sun is stationary in the cosmos; earth turns this way; the moon does this; and it takes 365¼ days for the earth to revolve around the sun. Then, all three will eventually line up so precisely that daylight will turn to night. Scientist tell us the next time we will witness this phenomenon in North America will be in about twenty years. ***IT's SCIENCE, BABY"!*** So, if it is as they say, why does the earth rotate at all?

When I began writing these essays (and I thank you for indulging me) it was because of some in the Catholic Church refused to give communion to Joe Biden. That spurred me to question the Church and its hierarchy—was I to be served by them or was I to wear a blindfold to be a Catholic? I read the Gospels looking for the words of Jesus to help answer the questions. It was a history lesson for me.

The essays became a vehicle for me to explore other things; does government work for me and you or just the select few? I wanted to communicate how we fail to help others and what needed to be done by us to fix it. Additionally, I wanted to know if there was a place for me in heaven given all the not so good things in my past.

Most of you know I don't evangelize or attempt to convince others to "take up their cross" and march on. I do question the prophets of the Old Testament mostly because of their apparent self-serving approach similar to many the evangelical leaders today. I prefer to listen to the words of Jesus to achieve my purpose. My goal from the start has always been to by a better human. Putting words on paper and sharing them with you forces me to work to achieve it.

When our family has a discussion on religion, and as you can imagine, it never goes well. The argument is framed around believing or not. As a believer, I find it difficult to understand why someone does not believe like me. I usually ask a simple question of the nonbeliever, "what if your wrong"; I never receive an answer.

Why is that? My guess is that we don't want to think about dying. It is not about whether we believe in God, it is about a state of nothingness after our last breath. Today, we are laughing and enjoying life and tomorrow there is no family or friends to spend time with is too much for us to contemplate.

When it's my time and you are there to bid me a farewell, if you hear someone saying, ". . . ashes to ashes and dust to dust . . .", get me out of there! Then, when it is your time, I will be waiting at the gate so that you will recognize a friend.

Yes, the Totality was spiritual. For me, it was affirmation that there is a God. Neither philosopher or scientist will convince me otherwise.

Essay 132

12 May 2024

Mother's Day

For the last several days I have been thinking of my mother. She has been gone for almost forty years, but it seems like I just stopped by and spent a little time with her. That's a good feeling. You see, I seldom missed visiting or talking on the phone with her every day. Some would characterize our conversations as the "same old thing" — day in and day out. That never bothered me; I wanted to hear her voice and make sure all was good.

Debbie likes to remind me of a conversation a long time ago she had with my sister. Jean called her and wanted to know if I was visiting that day. When Debbie confirmed it, my sister responded: "I'll wait until he leaves to scrub the floor." I never took off my shoes! My mother never cared though; she was happy to see me too.

The best analogy to describe my mother's physical stature comes from the movie "Rudy". The story was about a kid's dream to play football for Notre Dame. A character in the movie described him as "five foot nothing". That's my mother! That didn't matter though, she could deliver a punch. That punch took the form of a big stick — a four-foot yard stick. Besides not being three feet long, it wasn't your typical yard stick. It was about a half inch thick and three inches wide; had a million half-inch holes strategically spaced across the entire 48 inches! It may have been a promotional give-a-way from Fries. I can't say for sure if it came from Kenny's store, but I know this for sure, the designer was a diabolical sadist!

Here's a lesson for all, never make a mother mad when she has a big stick. I never had the courage to get a tattoo. One thing for sure, if I could look at my butt today there would be round tattoo-like circles still there!

In my eyes, my mother was perfect! That's all that matters to me. I was a jerk too many times. I was stupid too. I made mistakes. I made bad decisions. Through it all, my mother was there. She loved me unconditionally. I returned it and still do. Happy Mother's Day, Mum.

Essay 133

23 May 2024

Memorial Day

As I was thinking about writing this essay, a gentleman posted a thought about Memorial Day on a networking app a few days ago. His reflection on this day was a reminder of the reason we celebrate Memorial Day. He said, "[Memorial Day] is not a day to honor current military members for their service, Monday is set aside for those brave souls who lost their lives in defense of the freedoms you and I enjoy."

Other threads seemed to object to the singularity of the day. One in particular caught my attention. This man challenged the original premise of the post by making Memorial Day for all veterans that served our country in the military. Someone needs to tell him that is why we celebrate Veterans Day!

A second notable thread came from a lady moved by a funeral procession of a slain police officer. It is always tragic when a person is lost protecting you and me. We have days to honor fallen police officers. Every May 15th is National Peace Officers Memorial Day. Pennsylvania bestows the honor every May 6th. Ohioans pay their respect for slain officers on the 1st Thursday in May. Interpol pays tribute to the ultimate act of service every March 7 across the globe. No, Memorial Day is not to remember the bravery of a police officer, it is reserved exclusively for those killed serving our country in wartime.

A final thread I would like to share comes from a man bemoaning the change from May 30th to the 4th Monday in May. He implies the failure to recognize fellow Americans that died for us is because of an act of Congress almost 50 years ago moving some national holidays to a Monday and a 3-day weekend. Absurd!

Many people, including the aforementioned believe Memorial Day has changed. For me, it has been the same since the early 1950s. That's when I attended my first Memorial Day parade.

The holiday was important to me for a number of reasons. Growing up, it singled only a couple of weeks of school left before summer vacation. Next, was the excitement of the annual Memorial Day parade in West Newton. The revelers would form at the high school and march up 4th Street and turn left onto Main. The procession would stop at the plaque mounted on the wall of the bank building to pay homage to World War I veterans. The honor guard of the VFW, led by Bill Pritchard, would come to attention and salute their comrades. Behind "Pritch" in the formation was Ronnie Ulander, Babe Kelley, Jack Gibbons, Mike Weinhofer, Glen Ustazewski along with many more veterans. Tim Lander marched in a few parades too.

The high school band proudly joined the procession; Girl and Boy Scouts, Cub Scouts, and Little Leaguers. Local dignitaries' road in convertibles or classic cars. There were fire trucks. Bill McCauley would drive the big rig. The highlight for me was John Simon driving the antique fire engine.

As the parade paused on the bridge over the Youghiogheny to launch a wreath into the river to honor those lost at sea and the final marchers passed by, we followed them to the cemetery. Instead of lining up behind the last marchers, we took the shortcut along the P&LE tracks to the lower entrance of the sacred grounds.

As we arrived at the small amphitheater with a stage, folks gathered to hear the featured speaker for the day. Not me. It was a time to meet up with old friends not seen since last Memorial Day.

I take great pride in my hometown and the Avenue of Flags at the cemetery. Raising these flags in honor our deceased veterans is celebrating 30 years of service to the community. I am grateful to the many volunteers that make it possible.

Yes, Memorial Day is for remembering those that died to protect our way of life. For me, it is about honoring my dad and Uncle Ernie. It's about thinking about my friends' dads that served with distinction, but did not die fighting fascism. It is about comrades scared by mental and physical challenges because of their service.

I never liked when someone said to me, "thank you for your service". Maybe it is because I'm skeptical of their motive. Maybe it is because it is a little embarrassing. Next time when you feel the urge to thank a veteran, just smile and say hello. That's enough for us.

A patriot is someone that will lay it on the line for our freedom. Memorial Day celebrates that pledge.

Essay 134

13 June 2024

Father's Day

For Mother's Day I wrote about her. When the essay was about finished, I owed my dad the same respect, not because I wanted to keep things equal, but for it was long overdue. You see, in my family there was not a lot of hugs and kisses; I don't remember many affectionate verbal exchanges. That doesn't mean the family had a cold and detached relationship. Far from it. Seldom, maybe never, I said "I love you", but I sure felt it and do today.

In my Mother's Day tribute, I talked about a lady with a big stick, "The Enforcer"! My dad was the antithesis of an enforcer. Never did he paddle, yell, or discipline me. I think he was happy to let my mother do it!

My dad was proud of his service in the Army Air Corp during WWII. He was a veteran of the Pacific Theater and a proud member of the Thirteenth Army Air Force. The 13th was called the "Jungle Air Force". He was part of the island hopping that began for him in the Solomon Islands and continued through the Philippines. After the war, he remained in the reserves and returned to active duty for the Korean War. This time, he stayed stateside at Greenville Army Air Base in South Carolina.

He never liked talking about combat experiences. He did like to talk about his "buddies" and their shared experiences from the Southwest Pacific to Greenville. I remember one in particular that has remained with me for almost seventy years. During his postwar service, he and few local friends would make the trek from South Carolina to home often. There was no I-77 or I-79, only 2 lane roads. The clever sleuths would place aluminum strips in the hub caps of the car to confuse police radar. The image of Tobacco Road and Barney Fife sitting in his 1950 Ford along the road with a perplexing look on his face as the GIs sped by, makes me smile.

22 May 1983 was the darkest day of my life. That's the day he left us. I remember a doctor showing me an image of his chest. The bulge on his aorta looked the size of a football. He was transported to Shadyside and died during surgery. He previously had an aortic aneurysm repaired at Greensburg Hospital.

I often think of the choice he made to stay local for the first surgery. What if he would have gone to Pittsburgh for the repair? My kids—all of them—would have benefited from the chance to know their grandfather; and I know how grateful he would be for that opportunity. One thing sure, if you have a serious medical issue go to the best place available.

My dad was an auto mechanic. He was proud of his career choice. He had an opportunity to work for Convair, an aircraft manufacturing located in San Diago. California was too far from West Newton for my mother. He was asked to join Republic Steel at the Banning mine. He turned it down. He was a guy that like to work on cars.

Being good at what you do and working to get better every day is the lesson I learned from him. I hope my kids have the same principles my dad revered during his time on earth. When I am gone, my hope is for someone to say about me, just a "chip off the old block". There is no better epitaph for me.

My dad worked his butt off; six days a week, 10 hours a day for as long as I can remember. His compensation was small compared to people in offices and mills. It didn't matter to him. He like fixing cars and earned every penny (and more) of his paycheck. It took me a long time to understand chasing money wasn't the American dream. He understood that from the beginning.

When I went this way instead of that way, he never criticized, matter of fact, said nothing. I'm sure he had an opinion, but allowed me to figure things out.

My dad's goal was to live to 100. After all, he looked younger than his years and possessed the energy of a much younger person. Additionally, the genes he inherited from my grandmother made it a reasonable probability. However, the odds were against him. All those years on cold concrete floors, the constant battle with blood pressure, generational challenges, and multiple flare ups of gout made chances to be a centenarian unlikely.

I would like to close by sharing a story that defines him and his life. As my dad was about to be transported to the hospital for his final journey, he handed me his wallet for safe keeping. He said there was a lot of money in it. He was saving up to take my mother on a trip to Hawaii. My mother getting on an airplane to Hawaii? Only once she travelled outside 100 miles of West Newton and that was in the early 1950s! He wasn't deterred by her reluctance. After all, that was her dream. That was my dad, always thinking of his family.

By the way, the wallet had thirteen one-hundred-dollar bills in it!

"Be like Mike" was a Gatorade commercial featuring Michael Jordan, the greatest basketball player ever. The ad targeted young people with big dreams of being great—like Michael Jordan. All I ever want to do is "be like Mel".

Happy Father's Day, Dad.

Essay 135

12 August 2024

Choices

(A note to Jake, Buck, Nick, Jim and Max from Pap-Pap)

"The two most important days in your life are the day you're born and the day you find out why."[184] That was Mark Twin speaking.

Did you have a favorite teacher? Did that teacher inspire you? Imagine this scenario, you are intrigued by something a guest speaker said to your class. Did it motivate you to discover more? If I ask who is Robert Frost, will you know? If you do, the years in public education were well spent. If not, do you want me, or someone like me, to provide the answer? Well, it won't be me and I hope others tell you to look it up! Do you like poetry; have you ever read a poem and understood it? Many things to think about. Let me tell you why, but before I do, read *"Into My Own"* by Robert Frost.

"Into My Own"
By Robert Frost

A Boy's Will (1915)

One of my wishes is that those dark trees,
So old and firm they scarcely show the breeze,
Were not, as 'twere, the merest mask of gloom,
But stretched away unto the edge of doom.

I should not be withheld but that some day
Into their vastness I should steal away,
Fearless of ever finding open land,
Or highway where the slow wheel pours the sand.

I do not see why I should e'er turn back,
Or those should not set forth upon my track
To overtake me, who should miss me here
And long to know if still I held them dear.

They would not find me changed from him they knew—
Only more sure of all I thought was true.

Reading poetry is a challenge; sometimes it is outright baffling. Only after the poem is read, read again, digested a few times, and read a few more times will the poet's message come into focus. Perplexed; that's ok. Interpreting poetry is difficult. Ready to dig into the poem with me? Let's go!

"Into my Own" is a story of youthful exuberance in search of discovery. The speaker is Robert Frost. As he plans the escape from the life that is known, Frost shows concern for what lies ahead. The journey is filled with obstacles — a challenge that he may fail and be forced to abandon the odyssey. Frost muses;

---

[184] Mark Twain

if only these barriers can be conquered, then reaching a new beginning is possible. He decides the adventure is worth the risk and pursues the goal with courage and determination.

Family and friends are concerned his plan is ill-advised and tries to persuade him not to go. Regardless of the well-meaning resistance, he will not be deterred from reaching his potential. The next time all are together, he hopes they find him unchanged, but more confident in his beliefs.

That's my take on *"Into My Own"*; it's my opinion. Readers of poetry find their own meaning. Your interpretation carries the same weight as anyone. Remember, the world is full of opinions. Never forget. your opinion has value. Don't let anyone tell you otherwise, even you.

Are you bored; maybe disinterested? I can't blame you. I once was like you. I have an advantage over you though. I experienced *"Into My Own"* for the first time at age 76! Do I have regrets, sure? I will never know how things would have turned out if I would have sought my potential like you have the opportunity to do.

It's time for us to talk.

When an eighteen-year-old is forced to think about a time somewhere beyond tomorrow it brings no joy. After all, you are a young adult seeking independence and adventure. Family and friends are important to you; never would you do anything to hurt them, but it's time to make your own way.

There will be battles of will for sure with those you love and those that love you. It will be difficult for you to tell them: "No, this is what I want to do with my life". Will the plan be strong enough to convince others to hop on board and be part of the discovery of your full potential? Probably not, but remember, it is your plan!

Think back of your days in school. Kindergarten was scary at first. Do you remember looking at your parents with anxious eyes as a stranger said "Hello, my name is ______, follow me". That person was your teacher and ready to accompany you on an odyssey to discover all sorts of things. Did you know that? I doubt it. You were more concerned with surviving the day. Tomorrow and the next day would be better. New friends, lunchtime, and recess; could it be any more exciting? It could, and it will, but first, you will need to take the first few steps to the future.

You started the adjustment with respecting the teacher and others. How many times did the teacher say to you, "shush, Johnny is speaking ". Then, out of nowhere something happened, you began to add numbers, write sentences, create art, and make friends. School was becoming fun. School was an adventure! It never crossed your mind, but it was the beginning of your journey to the future.

You conquered kindergarten, Whoopee! Now it is summer break. You looked forward to it since Easter. Ballgames, swimming, a vacation; you could do almost anything. That is, as long as you didn't get in trouble. Remember when a well-meaning relative asked if you missed school. Taking a nano second to think, you hooted, "are you crazy"! A strange thing happened next. Yoda approached and mysteriously transported you to a dark place for no reason. That dark place was your room and the next hour seemed like an eternity.

Fast forward to August. The summer sun was blazing, but still a lot of time left for doing absolutely nothing. Yet, you were beginning to change. Suddenly, you remembered school would be starting in a couple of weeks. You were ready to go back; couldn't wait to see old friends from kindergarten. "Who will be my teacher?" "Will Johnny be in my class?" "Will I go out the same door for recess?"

The elementary school years passed like a blur. You had so much fun and made many friends. Chapter books looked daunting in 1st grade, but a breeze now. Those pesky word problems, well, they're easy-peasy. Mastering a game controller helped conquer the Chromebook. The iPad and games like Fortnite, Roblox, and Minecraft made you a critical thinker, a better decisionmaker, and look the part of an engineer. Not bad for a 12-year-old!

Next came middle school. Do you remember the time when the principal stopped you from running in the halls? Or, when the teacher told you to quit yelling to Johnny on the other side of the room? You thought, "being a teenager may not be all that fun!"

Changing classrooms after each period was cool. It was an opportunity to see other friends and forget about Napoleon and diagraming sentences. It may have seemed trivial to you at the time, but it was the school's way of forcing you to be responsible for personal actions. Three minutes to go from one place to the next, did you make it? Did the light bulb illuminate and learning became important to you?

With all the challenges of transitioning from a boy to a young man, you made it! By the time summer is over you will be a high schooler.

Did you think high school was the time to build a plan for the future or a time for more fun and a driver's license? For sure, it was a time for gaining knowledge to prepare to meet the future. You were beginning to "walk and chew gum" at the same time. Did you question school rules or social policies that seemed unreasonable? Did you take a stand for what is right? If you did, dissent is good as long as it has a solid foundation. You, alone know that answer. If you did all those things, the path to the future awaits.

Remember, core values will define you. These values are you. You will be measured by these values throughout your life.

If I could give one gift that remains with you for a lifetime it is this: "Do the right thing, not just do things right." I will share nugget of wisdom from Robert Frost poem.

> *"Two roads diverged in a wood, and I—*
> *I took the one less traveled by,*
> *And that has made all the difference."*[185]

Graduation Day is here and gone in a flash! What's next? For over a decade you have been preparing to seek your full potential. Did you know that? Remember the times a teacher forced you to learn Euclidean Geometry or introduced the "saddle curve" in Calculus? Did you struggle with superfluous concepts? I did, but got lucky. Geometry was a favorite subject for me in high school. Why, because of the teacher.

I was luckier than you. Calculus didn't make my life miserable until college. The "saddle curve" was a different animal among many abstract concepts. The teacher explain that the graph looked like a saddle for a horse. Ok, but why or what is it? More explanation followed with maxima, minima, and critical points being offered as help. I could calculate these points, but for what purpose? Then, someone told me the Golden Gate bridge was built using a "saddle curve" for the design of its towers, deck, and cables to make it safe. BINGO! Although the "why" remained fuzzy, but by relating it to something familiar helped me to the next discovery.

Do you confront challenges and move forward in a positive way? Or, do you just move forward?

It's time for us to get serious. Recall, I asked you many questions about your life up until the time of graduation from high school. The intent was to make you think and prepare for the future, not just to

---

[185] Frost, Robert. "The Road Not Taken", Mountain Interval, 1915

reminisce. It's not unusual for a young adult to not care much about preparing for the future. Here's a hard reality, it's time for you to start NOW! No excuses or procrastination. It is an opportunity to do it on terms set by you, not by another.

Something for you to chew on: "If you really want to do something, you'll find a way. If you don't, you'll find an excuse."[186]

During my time as a young adult, enlisting in the military was an option for anyone not prepared for the future. If I heard it once, I heard it a hundred times, "I'm not ready to make a lifetime decision, I'll wait to do it after my 4 years in the Service". Bullpucky!!! The time is now to begin the journey to the future.

Don't let others tell you that you are late and high school was the time to get ready for the future. We are humans with different clocks. I'm sure you know kids with a plan for their future all the way back to 9th grade. Good for them! That may have been you—maybe not. It's important to remember, IT'S NOT TOO LATE to start.

I hope you realize by now these words are my way of helping you do the right thing. To that end, the most important guidance I can give to you is this: MONEY IS NOT A MEASURE OF SUCCESS.

What's your options? College is today's "joining the military". Yet, it is a good option, but requires thought and consultation with others. What discipline is right for you? Do you have the resolve to commit to it while enduring objections? Are you willing to go to a place that provides the best preparation, not just good training? There will be opposition within your sphere of influence. Do you have the fortitude to remain resolute?

College is not the end-all to the future. It is not always the answer. Maybe a trade or vocation will lead to your full potential. Do you have the guts to hold back opposition? It is difficult for others that care about you to accept your decision. If you have the resolve and the right preparation, those that love you will support and encourage you.

People that love and care about you have a perception (call it a dream) for what is best for you. Nothing wrong with wanting the very best for you. However, the "very best" is what you believe it is.

The end of our conversation is here. The future requires discipline. If every venture is approached as an opportunity to be better tomorrow than today, then when you are old and look back, you will say, "I did ok".

"Did you hear that? There it is again. It's coming from that hill over there. Someone is calling my name." Hey, it's me, your Pap-Pap! Just checking in to make sure you are ok. I have said this many times before to you and to anyone within ear's reach, but just want you to know again how proud I am of you. You can't see me, but I'm smiling at you with great admiration.

Now, go find your potential.

---

[186] Jim Rohn; entrepreneur, author, and motivational speaker.

Essay 136

31 August 2024

Shameful

I read in the paper the other day someone said: "[The Presidential Medal of Freedom is] the highest award you can get as a civilian, it's the equivalent of the Congressional Medal of Honor." Continuing, "It's actually much better because everyone gets the Congressional Medal of Honor, they're soldiers. They're either in very bad shape because they've been hit so many times by bullets or they are dead".[187]

Who would have said such a stupid thing? It must have been Ilhan Omar. You know her. She's a Somali-born congresswoman from Minnesota and a founding member of "The Squad". No, it's not her. Then, it must be Robert Kennedy Jr. Remember, he was removed from the Instagram platform for sharing debunked falsehoods about the coronavirus and vaccines. Junior certainly is that stupid, but, no its not him.

Enough suspense, it's Donald! What a wicked human being. Trump uttered this nonsense as he praised Miriam Adelson, the widow of Republican mega-donor Sheldon Adelson and a recipient of the Medal of Freedom.

The backlash was swift. The National Commander of the VFW called the comment "asinine [and it] not only diminish the significance of our nation's highest award for valor, but also crassly characterizes the sacrifices of those who have risked their lives above and beyond the call of duty." Lipphardt double-downed on the criticism of Trump, "When a candidate to serve as our military's commander-in-chief so brazenly dismisses the valor and reverence symbolized by the Medal of Honor and those who have earned it, I must question whether they would discharge their responsibilities to our men and women in uniform with the seriousness and discernment necessary for such a powerful position."[188]

Senator Tammy Duckworth, a double amputee while fighting in the Iraq War, said: "Donald Trump is despicable. He doesn't deserve to be commander in chief. And certainly, those remarks are consistent with where he's always been. He thinks that we're suckers and losers. [Trump] is a five-time draft dodger who denigrates military men and women and our veterans and calls us suckers and losers . . ."[189]

Military veterans commented on these remarks on social media.[190] Here are a few posts:
- "Donald Trump insulting Medal of Honor recipients is just a continued trend of his disrespect towards our men and women in the military. It's disgusting. This is offensive on so many levels." **—Travis Ackers**

---

[187] LaPorta, James. "Trump says Medal of Freedom 'equivalent' to and 'much better' than Medal of Honor, sparking backlash from veterans", https://www.cbsnews.com/news/trump-medal-of-freedom-medal-of-honor/ , CBS News, 16 August 2024.

[188] Lipphardt, Al, National. "VFW Admonishes Former President for Medal of Honor Remarks", Veterans of Foreign Wars, Washington, DC, 16 August 2024. https://www.vfw.org/media-and-events/latest-releases/archives/2024/8/vfw-admonishes-former-president-formedal-of-honor-remarks

[189] Cohen, David. 'Tammy Duckworth rips Trump over remarks about medal-winning soldiers', Politico, 18 August 2024. https://www.politico.com/news/2024/08/18/tammy-duckworth-trump-soldiers-00174507

[190] Rahman, Khaleda, "Donald Trump's Medal Of Honor Remarks Spark Anger From Veterans", Newsweek, 16 August 2024. https://www.newsweek.com/donald-trump-medal-honor-remarks-spark-anger-veterans-miriam-adelson-1940135

- "Trump dishonor Medal of Honor recipients, our nation's highest military award for distinguished acts of valor. He deserves nothing but disdain and disqualifies himself from public office." —**Alexander S. Vindman**
- "F*ck this guy. He says the presidential medal of freedom he gave to one of his billionaire donors is better than the Medal of Honor, which is the highest military award, given for heroism in battle, often posthumously. Disgusting." — **Peter Henlein, Army veteran**
- Trump thinks the Medal of Honor is "secondary to the medal he gives his billionaire funders. He doesn't care about our military or their sacrifices." — **Veterans for Responsible leadership**
- "As a Marine, I can say that Trump is exactly right about the Medal of Honor. Getting that award means that either you or your friends and comrades came back in body bags or f***** up for life. No one should want that award." — **Joseph Lippincott, Trump supporter**

Criticizing the military and veterans with distinguished service is routine for Trump. Remember what he said about John McCain: "He's not a war hero . . . He's a war hero [be]cause he was captured. I like people that weren't captured, OK?"[191]

How about when he called service members "suckers and losers". Trump denied the report, but Jeffrey Goldberg (editor in chief of The Atlantic) cited four anonymous sources with firsthand knowledge. These comments were made as he canceled a visit to the Aisne-Marne American Cemetery near Paris in 2018 where Marines died in the battle of Belleau Wood during World War I. Trump said: "Why should I go to that cemetery? It's filled with losers."[192]

Or, how about Trump disparaging Gold Star families? The Vietnam Veterans of America, a non-partisan service organization that does not endorse or support political candidates, spoke out. The National President said, "we cannot remain silent when a Gold Star family member is being publicly denigrated. It is especially reprehensible when [an] individual is seeking to become the commander-in-chief of the Armed Forces of our nation. To lash out and disparage a family whose son gave his life defending this country is both shocking and disgraceful. And though Trump may never have spent a day in uniform, his disdain for the sacrifice of this young man and all who have made the ultimate sacrifice in defense of our Constitution is singularly un-American."[193]

It's been my modus operandi to provide my "2¢" after providing background for an essay. On this topic, there is nothing I can add beyond what I said earlier. It's perplexing how any veteran could still vote for Trump given his total contempt for military service.

Trump's criticism of uniformed service members falls on deaf ears of veterans supporting him. There has to be a breaking point with these veterans. That's wishful thinking on my part. The comment by the Marine earlier demonstrates that allegiance to the cult of Trump supplants "Duty, Honor, Country"[194] by too many veterans.

---

[191] Kaplan, Rebecca. "Trump: McCain only a war hero because he was captured", https://www.cbsnews.com/news/donald-trump-john-mccain-war-hero-captured/, CBS News, 18 July 2015.

[192] Segers, Grace and Gómez, Fin. "Trump denies report that he called service members 'losers' and CBS News 'suckers'", https://www.cbsnews.com/news/trump-military-service-members-losers-suckers-report/ , 4 September 2020.

[193] VVA: Trump's Attack on Gold Star Family Is Disgraceful and Un-American, https://vva.org/press-releases/vva-trumps-attack-on-gold-star-family-is-disgraceful-and-un-american/

[194] Douglas MacArthur to the cadets of the U.S. Military Academy on 12 May 1962.

On second thought, I do have "2¢" to share. The Census Bureau offers an interesting look at the military veteran electorate during the 2016 and 2020 general election.[195] [196]

In 2020, the veteran population in the United States was north of 18M. Four out of every five (79%) veterans registered to vote. The rate of registration for all citizens was 73%. The most intriguing revelation to me from the data was the number of registered veterans that actually voted—93% in 2020. Comparing that rate of participation to the actual vote (61%) in 2020 tells us veterans are more likely to fulfill their constitutional obligation than the rest of us.

In 2016, the number of veterans voting for Trump reflects the conservative leaning of the group and the gender of the candidates. The gap between Trump and Biden narrowed significantly in 2020. Some of the tightening came from the increase in voter turnout; more than 12% (17M). The fatigue with Trump contributed as did the likeability of Biden for the additional participation. I can't help but believe the criticism of John McClain and the disparaging of Gold Star families by Trump swayed some veterans.[197]

Baby Boomers and Generation X[198] are the most important veteran voting bloc and represent about 50% of all veteran voters in 2024. They favored Trump in 2016 and 2020 and likely to do the same this year. The margin of support will be in double-digits territory.

Could I be wrong and the outcome in 2024 look more like 2020 than 2016? Is it possible to draw even; maybe flip the script? It will take a Mazeroski swing of the bat for that to happen.

It's all about trends. Active-duty military is trending to the middle politically. Not long ago they were solidly Republican. The emergence of Gen Z and Millennials is probably responsible for the movement.

There is another dynamic taking shape. It is a fear for our freedom. As a veteran and the son of a veteran who defeated fascism with a bunch of buddies, veterans of all stripes understand (or should) the importance of fighting for these freedoms. That is trending now. At their core, veterans are patriot. Will they vote in the tradition of the seventy-seven patriots of a long time ago on the Lexington Green?

How will Trump's disparaging of veterans play out in 2024? We will see.

---

[195] U.S. Census Bureau, Voting and Registration in the Election of November 2016.

[196] U.S. Census Bureau, Current Population Survey, November 2020.

[197] National Center for Veterans Analysis and Statistics, Table 1L: Living Veteran Population and Projection

[198] Note. Gen: Z 1997-2012; Millennial 1981-1996; Gen X 1965-1980; Baby Boomer 1946-1964; Silent Generation 1928-1945; Greatest Generation 1901-1927. Identified are the top two generations for each age group.

Essay 137

31 August 2024

The Pledge

I wonder if Donald Trump and congressional Republicans realizes the original author of the *Pledge of Allegiance* was a socialist? Yes, it's true! In 1892, Francis Bellamy, a minister, penned what has become our loyalty oath. In the original form it read: "I pledge allegiance to my Flag and the Republic for which it stands, one nation, indivisible, with liberty and justice for all."

I can't blame "The Donald" (or his conspirators) for not knowing about Pastor Bellamy. After all, Trump attended the Wharton School at the University of Pennsylvania. Christian Socialism was not a part of the curriculum for the business school. For Trump and the rest of us, Christian Socialism blends Christianity and socialism and is based on the teachings of Jesus. Those that practice it believe social inequality results from the greed associated with capitalism.

Here are notable graduates of the Wharton School:
- **Michael Milken** - Inventor of high-yield bonds; convicted of securities violations and barred from the securities industry;
- **Elon Musk** - Co-founder and ex-CEO of PayPal, founder of SpaceX, CEO of Tesla Motors;
- **Mehmet Oz** – A "pitchman who repeatedly promoted products of questionable medical value"[199];
- **Donald Trump** – First former U.S. president to be convicted of a felony; and
- **Donald Trump Jr.** - Executive vice president of The Trump Organization.

Other graduates of Wharton School:
- **William J. Brennan Jr.** - Associate justice, US Supreme Court (1956-1990);
- **Warren Buffett** - CEO of Berkshire Hathaway;
- **William S. Paley** - Founder of CBS;
- **Frances Perkins** - Former U.S. Secretary of Labor, architect of Social Security system; and
- **William Wrigley Jr.** - Founder and CEO of Wrigley Company (gum and the Chicago Cubs).

Before I get back to the *Pledge*, did you know Michael Cohen at the bequest of Trump threatened to sue his high school, college, and the College Board if they released his grades. There is an interested account of Trump's days at Penn in the Philadelphia Magazine[200]. It's worth reading. Here's the link: (https://www.phillymag.com/news/2019/09/14/donald-trump-at-wharton-university-of-pennsylvania/)

In 1923, "*the Flag of the United States of America*" replaced "my Flag" in the original Pledge. In 1954, President Eisenhower encouraged Congress to add the words "*under God*" to it. The oath as it read today is: "*I pledge allegiance to the flag of the United States of America, and to the republic for which it stands, one nation under God, indivisible, with liberty and justice for all.*"

Thirty-one words that define what it is to be an American. We pledge *"to the flag"*, but it is more than a flag. It is a covenant among all to defend what is right and honorable as a citizen of the United States. It is to protect America against aggressors—foreign adversaries and domestic coups. It is to join with 330 million others to never allow anything to imperil the unity of purpose won almost 250 years ago in the

---

[199] Brian Slodysko and Marc Levy. "Dr. Oz made reputation as a surgeon, a fortune as a salesman", The Associated Press, 20 October 2022, https://apnews.com/article/dr-mehmet-oz-political-career-2022-midterm-f6ecd9ac9f0e95cda41193adc13c8437

[200] Valania, Jonathan. "*Fact-Checking All of the Mysteries Surrounding Donald Trump and Penn*", Philadelphia Magazine, 14 September 2019.

Commonwealths of Massachusetts, Pennsylvania, and Virginia; the states of New Jersey, New York, Vermont, Georgia, Carolinas, and Florida.

Internalizing the oath is to accept *"liberty and justice for all"*. The Revolutionary War was about rejecting a surrender of the right to self-determination; bow and curtsy to a king. We fought a civil war to keep the country whole. We fought world wars to defeat totalitarianism and remain free.

So, what happened?

Remember Essay #116, "Gifts of the Holy Spirit"? I wrote about White Rage and the fear of a power dynamic shift for these folks. Another name for it is "white backlash". Yes, it is about Jim Crow, but has morphed into a more general form of envy called "white grievance". It simple terms, it is a dark response by some white people to racial progress or ethnic groups perceived as privileged over them. Make no mistake, White grievance is a force in America politics.

The wrath of white grievance is not limited to people of color or those speaking little or no English. You and I are targets of these small-minded folks too. Do you work hard, received merit promotions, and save for the future? Did you help your kids with their homework? Do you go to church? Do you follow moral and ethical codes? If you do these things and had a successful life, you must be privileged like black and brown people.

The grieved people in our country are Trump people. They are the cult of Trump. The followers of Trump drink the tonic brewed by the cult leader. The ingredients are simple—lies, lies, and more lies; human hatred; fear peddling; and "Jim and Jamie" Crow. So much more to say, but so little time left.

 In 2016, I couldn't imagine enough people would vote for Trump and make him president. I was wrong. After four exhausting years including his response to a global health crisis that ended up killing millions of Americans that did not have to die, I was sure he would lose. I was right. In 2024, I feel like 2020. Hope I'm not wrong.

I spend too much time trying to figure out why anyone did or will vote for Trump. I mentioned the COVID crisis and his handling of it. I, and probably you too, never expected a President of the United States to suggest we drink bleach to kill a virus. At the time, we all laughed at Trump's idiocy. The disgusting part for me is how many people actually tried it.

Trump taking highly classified documents from the White House for personal use is criminal. During my time with NSA, the consequence was made clear to me for doing as he did. A federal judge, appointed by him, has done everything to keep him from judgement day. Let me say that again, a federal judge with the duty to uphold the laws of the United States and the Constitution is doing the bidding for Trump.

There are so many actions and accusations against Trump. Nothing compares to the coup he orchestrated against our democracy. It is shameful and rises to a "high crime and misdemeanor" against the people of the United States of America. No punishment is too severe for him.

In Essay #136 –"Shameful", I wrote about how military veterans vote for Trump. If you recall, this group supported Trump in large numbers. Read the "Oath of Enlistment"[201] for United States military personnel below, then tell me how active military and service veterans could consider voting for him.

---

[201] Source: U.S. Army Center of Military History; (Title 10, US Code; Act of 5 May 1960 replacing the wording first adopted in 1789, with amendment effective 5 October 1962).

"I, ______, do solemnly swear (or affirm) that I will support and defend the Constitution of the United States against all enemies, foreign and domestic; that I will bear true faith and allegiance to the same; and that I will obey the orders of the President of the United States and the orders of the officers appointed over me, according to regulations and the Uniform Code of Military Justice. So help me God."

The enlisted oath contains the passage, "... I will obey the orders of the President of the United States and the orders of the officers appointed over me ..." It is important to note that 'orders' means "lawful orders"!

A commissioned officer swears to a similar oath. Their promise includes "I will support and defend the Constitution of the United States against all enemies, foreign and domestic ..."

A final thought about a Trump supporter: when a person votes for Trump, it's less of an indictment on him, but speaks to the values of the person casting the vote.

Let me conclude with the oath[202] of office for the President of the United States: "I do solemnly swear (or affirm) that I will faithfully execute the office of President of the United States, and will to the best of my ability, preserve, protect and defend the Constitution of the United States."

---

[202] Source: Article II, Section 1, The Constitution of the United States

Essay 138

1 September 2024

Participation Trophy

I like rewarding kids for taking part in anything. I don't care if its baseball, golf, chorus, zoo camp; you name it, I'm for it. Unfortunately, there are many that disagree with me. The naysayers will not change me, I still like seeing the smile on a nine-year-old when the coach gives him a trophy for being part of the team.

That brings me to the Presidential Medal of Freedom. This award evolved over time, call it morphed if you choose, but what Trump did by elevating it above the Medal of Honor, well, it's just plain disgusting. The original intent was good and honorable. It's not anymore. Before I go down that path, let's look at when and how it began.

President Truman established the Medal of Freedom 1945.[203] The intent was to recognize extraordinary service in defeat of the Axis[204] during World War II. The meritorious act could not be performed within the continental United States. Later, Truman expanded (1952) the original executive order.[205] The award was to enhanced to include national emergencies with potential impact on the security of the United States as worthy of consideration. Additionally, the name of the award was changed to the "Presidential Medal of Freedom".

The first American citizen to receive the Medal of Freedom was Anna Rosenberg (1945). She immigrated to the U.S. from Hungary in 1902 and became a citizen in 1919. Rosenberg served as the regional director for the War Manpower Commission[206] (1942) and as the special envoy to Europe for Roosevelt and Truman.[207]

John F. Kennedy made the final changes to the award in 1963.[208] The purpose of the executive order was to modernize the language for the award. Also, the criterion for the award was expanded to include "cultural or other significant public or private endeavors". However, the key change was to give the sitting president the juice to select the recipient.

President Kennedy's original intention was to recognize contributions in the arts and academia along with public service. Because of the vagueness of the standard, the type of achievement broadened eligibility by adding athletics, business, civil rights, religion and more. Regardless of the motive, the award, once to recognize achievement to protect the United States from aggressors, has mutated into transactional politics.

---

[203] EXECUTIVE ORDER 9586, "The Medal of Freedom".

[204] An alliance of Germany, Italy, and Japan during WWII.

[205] EXECUTIVE ORDER 10336, 3 April 1952.

[206] A federal agency charged with planning/regulating the labor needs of agriculture, industry, and the armed forces during World War II.

[207] Little, Becky. *"The Presidential Medal of Freedom Began as a World War II Honor"*, A&E Television Networks, 6 February 2020. https://www.history.com/news/presidential-medal-freedom-truman.

[208] EXECUTIVE ORDER 11085.

In an article in the New England Journal of Political Science in 2015 entitled, *"The Politics of the Presidential Medal of Freedom: A Fifty-Year Analysis, 1963-2013"*[209], authors from various academic disciplines explored the awarding of the Medal by ten presidents. They concluded:
1. Presidents use the medal to shape their legacy;
2. To garner support among various constituency groups;
3. To achieve high-priority goals;
4. To communicate a vision of ideal civic contribution; and
5. To provides insight regarding a president's values, preferences, and motivations.

It's time to discuss how Trump viewed and chose recipients for the Presidential Medal of Freedom. Robert Schlesinger, a veteran Washington journalist and commentator, wrote an essay for THINK[210] in 2018. The essay, *"Trump giving Miriam Adelson the Medal of Freedom captures the transactional nature of his presidency[211]"*, Trump's vanity is always on full display — 'If you do this for me, I will do this for you'.   It's not what JFK envisioned for the award. Remember, Trump is not Kennedy!

Schlesinger wrote: "Freedom may be priceless, but the Presidential Medal of Freedom may have a price tag — $133 million." That's how much Miriam and Sheldon Adelson, the Republican megadonors, ponied up to conservative groups and candidates in the 2016 presidential campaign and the 2018 election cycle.   Trump was the leading beneficiary ($20 million) of their money. The Center for Public Integrity reported the Adelsons ranked 2nd in money given to Trump's presidential run.

Schlesinger: "It pays to play. Not only is Miriam Adelson getting the medal, but Trump personally lobbied Japanese Prime Minister Shinzo Abe on Sheldon Adelson's behalf for a casino license."

Schlesinger offered and update to his essay. *The Washington Post reported on January 31, 2019 that the Adelsons additionally gave $500,000 to a legal fund for Trump aides on October 1, 2018.*

Quid pro quo!

Schlesinger closed with the following: "Speaking of the arts center which would come to bear his name, John F. Kennedy said in 1962: 'After the dust of centuries has passed over our cities, we, too, will be remembered not for victories or defeats in battle or in politics, but for our contribution to the human spirit.' Except for Miriam Adelson, who will be remembered for her contributions to Donald Trump."

What is Miriam Adelson's "especially meritorious contribution to the security or national interests of the United States, or world peace or cultural or other significant public or private endeavor?"
- As a doctor, Miriam Adelson specializes in drug addiction. In 1993 she founded a substance abuse center and research clinic at Sourasky Medical Center in Tel Aviv, Israel and in 2000 the Adelsons opened the Dr. Miriam and Sheldon G. Adelson Research Clinic in Las Vegas, Nevada.

---

[209] Kopko, Kyle C.; McClellan, E. Fletcher; Devine, Christopher J.; Casey, Jillian E.; and Ward, Julia L., *"The Politics of the Presidential Medal of Freedom: A Fifty-Year Analysis, 1963-2013"* (2015). Political Science Faculty Publications. 98. https://ecommons.udayton.edu/pol_fac_pub/98

[210] THINK is NBC News' home for op-eds, in-depth analyses and essays about news and current events.

[211] Schlesinger, Robert. *"Trump giving Miriam Adelson the Medal of Freedom captures the transactional nature of his presidency"*, THINK: Opinions, Analysis, Essays)NBC News), 16 November 2018; Updated 2 February 2019. https://www.nbcnews.com/think/opinion/trump-giving-miriam-adelson-medal-freedom-captures-transactional-nature-his-ncna937121

- May 2024: $1M contribution to Truth and Courage PAC supporting Senator Ted Cruz.
- Bloomberg reported: $90M to Trump for 2020 election
- Newsweek reported: $25M direct to Trump's 2016 campaign; Adelsons gave $424M to Republicans since 2016
- Open Secrets reported: Total of $170M+ to Republicans in 2020.

A research clinic in Las Vegas and a substance abuse center in Tel Aviv certainly fall within the "other significant public or private endeavor". But, that's not why Adelson received the award. Trump's only vision of service is what can you do for him.

Trump, like so many of the things he touches, destroys what is good about things. The Presidential Medal of Freedom is forever tainted for past and future recipients. The noble intention of Truman and Kennedy to honor "meritorious contribution to the security or national interests of the United States" has been devalued beyond recovery.

It's time to return to something that matters—trophies—participation trophies!

Recently, there has been a lot of criticism (and support) to giving a kid a trophy for participating in something. Here's a sampling of what is being said about it.

In Favor of . . .

- Stress teamwork and individual growth over winning
- Contributes to an inclusive environment
- Good for a kid's emotional health
- Encourages kid to join in fun activities
- Kids know it is not the same as winning a championship

Oppose to . . .

- Discourage hard work
- Undervaluing competition
- Discourage playing to win
- Takes away the motivation to improve
- Make kids think they are winner when they are not

The critics did nothing to change my mind. We have a box—a big box—of trophies earned by Diane, Jack, and Bob. The kids haven't looked at these trophies in more than thirty years. I know if we asked them, they would say get rid of them. I would be ok with that. A piece of hardware will never take that smile from their face that will remain burned in my memory forever.

One last thought about the Presidential Medal of Freedom. The Medal has become a trophy for participation and not in a good way. The critics of participation trophies were right. They discourage hard work and stymie success; they take away motivation to be better; and, above all, make a kid (Trump) believe he is a winner!

Essay 139

12 August 2024

The Road Not Taken

By Robert Frost

Two roads diverged in a yellow wood,
And sorry I could not travel both
And be one traveler, long I stood
And looked down one as far as I could
To where it bent in the undergrowth;

Then took the other, as just as fair,
And having perhaps the better claim,
Because it was grassy and wanted wear;
Though as for that the passing there
Had worn them really about the same,

And both that morning equally lay
In leaves no step had trodden black.
Oh, I kept the first for another day!
Yet knowing how way leads on to way,
I doubted if I should ever come back.

I shall be telling this with a sigh
Somewhere ages and ages hence:
Two roads diverged in a wood, and I—
I took the one less traveled by,
And that has made all the difference.

During the early part of the 20TH century, Robert Frost spent time in England and became friends with Edward Thomas[212]. Frost and Thomas would take long walks together. One day, as they were walking, they came across two roads. Thomas was uncertain which road to take and later would regret not taking the other road; hence, the inspiration for "The Road Not Taken".

The poem's structure has a rhyme scheme of ABAAB[213]. What would my high school teachers say of me when I wrote about the structure and rhyme pattern of a poem? Mrs. Stricker (11th grade English) would ask, "whose paper did you copy?" while Miss Neff (12th POD and Intro to Research) is smiling! Why the difference in their opinion of me? One teacher saw a bespectacled skinny kid from Bull Run with nowhere to go and the other saw potential in me.

The metaphorical significance of the poem is the decision-making all of us are force to endure during our lifetime. These decisions range from trivial to life-altering. Most of our choices are somewhere in-between; however, all come with consequences.

---

[212] Philip Edward Thomas was a British writer of poetry and prose.

[213] ABAAB is a rhyme scheme that is used in poems and songs to indicate which lines rhyme with each other.

There are a few lines I would like to discuss from the poem. The first is from the second stanza—
"*Because it was grassy and wanted wear*". As Frost scanned the options, he was intrigue by the
challenge of the unknown and the adventure of the pursuit.

Do you remember when it was your turn to be the 'big dog' in high school? That was your senior
year! The guidance counselor called all seniors together and separated into two groups; college-bound
and career-ready. For the latter group, opportunities were abundant. The local car dealer was in serious
need of a salesperson. Kraynek's was looking for a butcher. Steel mills were hiring. Looks like the
decision to launch a career without more education was right for them.

Seniors planning for college were filling out applications for Harvard, Yale and even the University of
Hawaii. Others were dreaming of careers from doctors, lawyers, and more. Some were fantasizing about
glamorous pursuits after college.

All seniors were ready for their next journey. To follow an uncharted path becomes an adventure and, at
the same time, exhilarating. It never entered their brain the way forward is not without obstacles. Good
times turn to bad. Mills layoff. Colleges reject applications. Dreams of working as a translator at the
United Nations never happens. How we manage these adversities make all the difference.

"*I shall be telling this with a sigh*" is the first line of the final stanza. To 'sigh' is a metaphor for an
emotion. Is Frost demonstrating regret or disappointment in his choice? Or, is it simply fatigue by the
process? Maybe it is satisfaction in the choice. Regardless of the reason, it offers us a chance to
understand the complexity of making a decision with substantial impact on our life.

Frost was right when he wrote: "*I took the one less traveled by, and that has made all the difference*".
We interpret these lines as validation of the poet's choice. What if it was not? Frost acknowledged that
possibility early in the poem. If we do as Frost did, then the choice becomes our fate. If there is regret in
the decision, playing the "coulda", "woulda, "shoulda" game is a waste of good energy.

The poem is the most read (and favorite of many of us) of the poetry of Robert Frost. For me, I can relate
to it in my career choices. I trained to be a math teacher. Why, because it was what I did best, not great,
but best when considering other attributes of mine. I was passionate about teaching math to kids, but
abhorred the other parts of the profession. Those 'other parts' were as a disciplinarian, a lunch room
supervisor, a study hall monitor, being patient with parents and that sort of stuff. If I could have worked
in my little bubble of just teaching math, things would have been peachy. That wish was as unrealistic as
being the shortstop for the Pittsburgh Pirates. I needed to find out what was my passion and how to
achieve it.

Eventually, I found it. It was simple in retrospect. I needed to have 'dirt under my fingernails' to be
happy. The dad of a girl from high school helped me get there. How many math teachers chose to work
in a coal mine? I only know of one. Turns out, I found my passion. Unfortunately, the coal industry, at
least in Pennsylvania, dried up. Time for another career decision.

In 1987, I was offered a job with Standard Oil in Columbus, Ohio. It was a good job with exciting career
potential. The downside was leaving the only place I called home. The forces working on me to provide
for our family were powerful. It's part of my DNA to take care of those most important to me. The new
job provided that continuity. We eventually settled in Dublin. It was a good place for our family. The
problem for me, it was not West Newton. Back to choices.

Regrets are a part of life. Dwelling on them is counter to the advice of Frost. When a decision is made there is no looking back. We proceed with vigor and full-throttle. If our path happens to be is blocked, pursuing the next opportunity requires the same energy.

Frost lamented, *"Two roads diverged in a yellow wood, and sorry I could not travel both"*. Sorry Mr. Frost you couldn't explore both roads. Fortunately, I did *"And that has made all the difference"*.

Essay 140

22 September2024

Our Life

My original intent with this essay was to become a "time traveler" and look back at the eight decades I have occupied a small part of the cosmos. Early on, it became apparent to me that this pursuit was not mine along, but all the folks born in the second half of the 20th century. Time for the journey.

1950s – "Fabulous Fifties"

Timex watch; black & white TVs; Scran Wrap; polio vaccine; poodle skirts; sideburns; Hula Hoop; diners & jukeboxes; Drive-in Theaters; Letterman sweater; Civil Defense drills; Pompadour & Poodle hairstyles; telephone booths; shopping malls; transistor radios.

1960s – "Psychedelic 60s"

Selma; Vietnam; JFK, MLK, RFK; Afros; Barbie dolls; The Beatles; Go-Go boots; miniskirts; tie dye T-Shirts; flower power; hippies; psychedelic drugs; groovy; Mazeroski; love beads; peace signs; The Twist; Arnold Palmer; UT Clock Tower sniper; color TVs.

1970s – "Me Decade"

Vietnam; Watergate; internet; cell phone; Microsoft; bell-bottoms; Saturday Night Fever; Nixon; pet rock; All in the Family; Steel Curtain; Three Mile Island; Apple.

1980s – "Greed Decade"

AIDS; MTV; Pac-Man; Hip-Hop; Cheers; Berlin Wall; Sally Ride; Mount St. Helens; John Lennon; Challenger; Chernobyl; Supreme Court female justice; Mario Lemieux.

1990s – "Technology"

Fanny packs; Nintendo; smart phone; Soviet Union; Gulf War; Waco; MP3s; OJ; beepers; boy bands; Forest Gump; OKC bombing; Columbine; Google.

2000s – "Google it!"

911; Shanksville; Obama; reality TV; iPods; Y2K; YouTube; Facebook; iPhone; Apollo 11; Livestrong; Iraq War; Virginia Tech; Enron; War on Terror; Sydney Crosby.

We began the journey innocently. The 50s were carefree and mostly a time to vegetate. The 60s ushered in political assassinations and war. Our government liked to call Vietnam a conflict. By any stretch of the imagination, it was a war. Ask the families and friends of 58,000 guys and gals on the Wall in D.C. Don't forget the GIs maimed by that war.

Gary Markle, a classmate of mine, was one of the more than 150,000 wounded in Vietnam.[214] Gary died on 28 September 1996. Visit Gary's page (https://www.vvmf.org/Honor-Roll/1153/GaryMerleMarkle/) on the *In Memory Honor Roll* of the Vietnam Veterans Memorial Fund website. Gary was inducted to the honor roll in 2005. There is exactly one remembrance posted for him—me! I'm ashamed of me and others that knew him for not taking the time to remember.

The youth of America knew Vietnam was wrong. Our politicians did not. The disconnect launched a movement that changed our country forever.

---

[214] Defense Causality Analysis System (DCAS), https://dcas.dmdc.osd.mil/dcas/app/conflictCasualties/vietnam/vietnamSum, accessed 12Sep2024.

"The Me Decade", a phrase coined by Thomas Wolfe[215], concerned the shift from social and political justice to a more selfish focus on individual well-being by Baby Boomers. The economic challenges of the 1970s along with political corruption highlighted by Watergate contributed to the self-centric attitude. Baby Boomers, once idealistic, turned to more practical matters of family and career creating a void filled by egocentricity.

The decades from the 80s through the early 21st century is characterized by change. From technology to mass casualty acts; to terrorism everywhere; to a climate crisis; to a black man becoming president. Navigating these times were a challenge.

Sometimes, I long for a return to the 50s. It was a comfortable time. Neighbors actually liked each other. We were there to help during tragedies. When we got a little extra pay for our effort, it was time to celebrate.

Enough of this reminiscing, it's time to face our current challenges head-on.

The decade we live in began by forcing us to confront a world-wide pandemic that killed millions. Grading our government's initial response would be a "D-". When Biden arrived on the scene things changed and the government did what governments exist to do. That kind of involvement earns an A^{+}. Placing a grade on the people that willfully obstructed measures (masks, vaccination, isolation) to defeat COVID disrespects grading systems. They are evil, pure evil.

 How can a convicted felon run for president? A better question, how can any American vote for Trump? Imagine for a moment, Eisenhower, wanting a 3rd term; engineered a coup to get his way. Never would have happened. Ike was a patriot. Next, imagine Nixon doing the same thing. Never would have happened. As much as I detest Nixon, he sided with country over self.

I used to be an MSNBC junky, After Biden was elected, I switched channels to Pittsburgh sports. Recently, I began to tune in to the progressive network to lift my spirits a little on a bad day. One night, Alex Wagner had a pollster from the New York Times on to discuss a segment of the electorate that remains undecided about the candidates for president. The group seems to be a single-issue voter, their current economic status. They are mostly Gen Z[216] folks from all backgrounds willing to vote their wallet rather than values.

Gen Z is believed to be the best hope for us. They value diversity and are more analytical than previous generations. Gen Z is pragmatic and use dialogue to solve conflicts. A "Zer" believes human activity is responsible for global warming. Their politics are progressive and acknowledge minorities are treated less fairly than whites; they believe LGBT is good for the community.

So why is some of Gen Z considering voting for Trump? They are aware of the division he pursues and the hate he speaks. Trump's policies are in direct contrast to what the generation believes. So why? My answer: the generation is becoming the "New Me Decade" from the 1970s. I hope I'm wrong.

With all the justifiable fear for our democracy, I came upon something Abraham Lincoln said to Congress in 1862. He called America "the last best hope of earth".[217] We need Gen Z to step up.

---

[215] An American novelist, journalist, and social commentator.

[216] Gen Z: b.1997-2012

[217] Lincoln, Abraham. President of the United States, Annual Message to Congress, 1 December 1862.

Essay 141

23 May 2024

I am a Good Shepherd

For Jake, Buck, Nick, Jim, and Max

Jesus said, *"I am the good shepherd . . . I know mine and mine know me . . . I will lay down my life for the sheep."* [218]

Jake, Buck, Nick, Jim, and Max; these are my "sheep". I want to be their rock. I want to be there during their darkest hour and share in their greatest triumph. I want to listen to their most trivial thoughts. I want to laugh at their jokes. I want cry when they do. I want to learn from them. I want to be there the moment they accept doing the right thing is who they want to be. Most of all, I want them to like me.

Jesus gave his life for us. I would give mine for Jake, Buck, Nick, Jim, and Max.

In an essay to my dad, I shared his view on life especially how long he hoped to be on this earth. I interpreted his wish as remaining alive for as long as possible. Now, I believe he was telling me that he wanted to be there to be with his kids.

My dad had three grandchildren; I have five. He died a few days short of his sixty-ninth birthday; I am about to be seventy-seven. I can only imagine how pleased he would have been for an extra eight years.

I'm no different than my dad. I want to live a long time for the same reason. I'm sure he did the math to come up with living to 100. I did too. I will be ninety-two when Max graduates from high school. That would make Jake twenty-four; Buck, Nick, and Jim would be somewhere in between. 92? Nope! Not long enough. Then, what is the magic number? I want to live long enough to be called "great Pap-Pap!

---

[218] **[Jn 10:11,14-15]**

Essay 142

28 August 2024

I Found My Purpose

Never thought about a purpose for my life. I meandered through life taking it a day at a time. As opportunities or challenges came my way, I accepted the outcome and called it fate. In retrospect, I was too lazy to find my purpose. That's the sum total of my existence on earth until a few years ago. Before sharing how I found my purpose, let me offer how fate has impacted me.

When it was time for me to come home from the Far East, I expected orders to report to Fort Meade in Maryland. After all, I worked for NSA and its headquarters is there. Instead, I was sent to San Antonio. Disappointed was a mild description of my emotions. Some would say it was fate that sent me to Texas.

During my time overseas, I became friends with a family from Kansas. The Knightly's advised me to let that pesky fate take care of things. The advice did little to consol me. Turns out, six months into my stay in San Antonio, orders showed up in my mail box to report immediately to Fort Meade. Just maybe there is something to that fate thing!

Fate is not purpose, it made me start looking for my place before I turn into dust.

 I spent the good part of six decades searching for it. My twenties were dedicated to making up for lost time and full of play and more play. The 1980s for me was adjusting to one, two, then three kids. I was "old" by parental standards, but Debbie was there to keep me straight and centered for the next challenge. God knew I need her. Could it have been fate?

My forties and fifties were about work and career; never had time to think about purpose. The new century brought a strong desire to retire. After all, Fred, John, and Tim among others packed it in. A few years later, and before I was ready, fate showed up and I joined my friends.

Since we left West Newton in 1987, I was planning a return someday. Well, you know what is said about the best man-made plans—a woman has the power to veto them. Debbie was very emphatic when she said, "I'm not going anywhere as long as the grandkids are in Ohio." So, Medina is where we hang our hat. That is, unless I can talk the kids into moving to Pennsylvania! Here's hoping fate can do its magic.

An article in the Harvard Business Review defined purpose "as an overarching intention that is personally meaningful and of consequence to the world beyond yourself".[219] Roger Allen, a counselor and life coach, agrees and adds, "[purpose] connect you with something bigger than yourself".[220] Finding purpose in life is to contribute to the greater good of humanity. (That's me defining it.) All make sense, but it's too much of a macro approach for me. If I am going to find my purpose, it's going to find me first. That's exactly what happened four years ago.

 When Jim was born in 2019, Bobby was forced to move in with us. I used the word "forced" because it wasn't his first choice by any stretch of the imagination and not ours either. Debbie and I expected to do what other empty-nesters do; travel, spend time with the grandkids (and send them home after a while), or simply do nothing if we choose. That wasn't in the cards for us.

---

[219] Ayse Yemiscigil, Melis Sena Yılmaz, Matthew T. Lee. "How to Find Your Purpose", Havard Business Review, 15 September 2023.

[220] Roger K. Allen. Ph.D. Blog, "Defining Your Purpose", https://www.rogerkallen.com/defining-your-purpose/

Bob was a single parent with a job. Jimmy needed all the things a newborn requires. Jake was old enough for preschool. The pressure on Bob was overwhelming. He became the provider, the mother and father, the cook, the bather, the counselor, a fighter for custody and more. For all the right reasons, Bobby sold his house and moved in with us. Debbie and I understood the challenges for him and opened the door wide. Our home—the home of Diane, Jack, Bob, Libby and Maggie would now be the home of Jake and Jim too.

Debbie and I would never be confused with *Ozzie and Harriet*. Our family certainly could not be mistaken for the *Cleavers* or the *Cunninghams*. For me, I was Robert Young in *Father Knows Best*, not in a good way. We were not the *Waltons*; maybe more like the *Clampetts*. Debbie was our *Edith Bunker*, in a good way. For all the trials and tribulations, we are making it.

It's been more than four years now. Debbie and I would not change a minute of it. Along with the challenges, it's been the best years of our life. The dream of travel and carefree living never comes up. We are comfortable with how things have turned out. We are actually very grateful for everything.

I often tell others that the grandkids are my way of atoning for being a less than perfect father. But it is so much more than that. When Jim said to me for the first time "I want go to **OUR** house", there are no words to describe my feelings. As I write about it now, it still brings tears to my eyes. I am comfortable in saying it will always do that to me.

I help Jake with his math homework. He really doesn't need much, but it's good for me and I hope it is the same for him. He gets a little frustrated with me when I encourage him to check every answer. Someday, Jake will reap the fruit from tedium of his labor; it's my way for him to pay attention to details. So much of what I do is to make him a critical thinker.

Little things mean the most to me. When Jake is about to get on the school bus, he takes one last look at me with the most beautiful and adoring eyes. Or, when Jim and I are walking down the street and he reaches for my hand. Or, when Jake wakes up in the morning and greets me with an incredible approving smile. Or, when Jimmy says, "I love you Pap-Pap". I could go on and on.

A heart breaks because of true love. I want to share a time it happened to me. Jake experienced respiratory distress one Sunday evening. He was four or five at the time. Bobby took him to the ER and he was rushed to Akron Children's Hospital by ambulance. Turns out it was an asthma attack. After a few days he came home with a band-aid covering the IV blood draw site on his arm. I started to remove it and he began to cry frantically. Jake thought if the band-aid was removed all his blood would drain out.

Jake's fear became my heartache. Never in my life had I experienced something so personally painful. It is burnt into the retina of my eyes for eternity. I pray that Jake or Jim or Buck or Nick or Max will never be asked to confront a fear like that day.

If all the kids remember one thing from our time together it would be, regardless of the challenge, always do the right thing. That is my wish for them.

You know, I really like Jake and Jim.

I found my purpose for sure. After years of wondering if there was a purpose for me on this earth, I found it in two of the most extraordinary kids.